How to Be Less Socially Anxious

How to Be Less Socially Anxious

Practical Skills to
Stop Overthinking, Be Confident,
and Thrive in Social Situations

Megan Ashley Smith, LCMHC, NCC

ZEITGEIST · NEW YORK

Published in the United States by Zeitgeist™
An imprint and division of Penguin Random House LLC
1745 Broadway, New York, NY 10019
penguinrandomhouse.com
zeitgeistpublishing.com

Zeitgeist™ is a trademark of Penguin Random House LLC.
ISBN: 9780593886243

Cover art © by ulimi/Getty Images
Book design by Erin Yeung
Edited by Kim Suarez

Printed in the United States of America
The authorized representative in the EU for product safety and compliance is
Penguin Random House Ireland, Morrison Chambers, 32 Nassau Street, Dublin D02 YH68, Ireland. https://eu-contact.penguin.ie
1st Printing

I proudly dedicate this book to myself,

and to all that I've accomplished

in my journey

Contents

Introduction

My challenges with social anxiety began in my teenage years, when the constant fear of being watched and judged made even the most minor interactions feel overwhelming. I'd avoid eye contact in class, avoid making new friends, and often found excuses to skip social events with the friends I did have. These fears kept me from connecting with others and enjoying life to the fullest. Over the years, I've dedicated myself to understanding and overcoming social anxiety, learning from both mental health experts and my journey.

Social anxiety can be incredibly isolating, causing you to avoid social situations, exhibit physical symptoms such as sweating and trembling, and generate negative thoughts and self-talk.

But here's the hopeful truth: Change is possible.

As both a therapist and a person with social anxiety, I've spent years learning from mental-health experts, connecting with people who share similar struggles, and dedicating my time and work to providing practical solutions. Techniques like mindfulness and setting small, achievable goals can help reduce anxiety by helping us manage distress, regulate emotions, and challenge negative thought patterns that keep us stuck.

Overcoming social anxiety is not an overnight process. It requires patience, persistence, and support from others. However, every step you take toward facing your fears is a victory. You can build confidence and resilience by learning to accept and manage anxious feelings. My mission is to guide you on this journey by offering the tools and encouragement needed to transform those anxious moments into confident strides.

How to Use This Book

Think of this book as a road map for better understanding yourself and your relationship to others. There will be time to reflect, analyze, and take action. Here's how you can make the most of it:

Start with **Understanding Social Anxiety.** This introductory section provides a clear picture of what social anxiety is—and what it isn't. It will help you recognize the symptoms and underlying causes, laying a strong foundation for your progress.

Part I equips you with practical skills to work through your anxious feelings. You'll discover key self-care practices and techniques to stop overthinking and start communicating more confidently. These skills are designed to empower you, offering simple, effective ways to take control of your anxiety.

Part II dives into real-life social situations that often feel overwhelming. Here, you'll find step-by-step guidance on applying the skills from Part I to these scenarios, allowing you to practice and build your confidence.

For the best results, I recommend starting with Part I to fully grasp and practice the skills before moving on to the specific situations in Part II. However, this book is designed to be flexible to meet your needs. If you feel more comfortable jumping directly to specific situations that most concern you, and working backward from there, that's perfectly fine.

Setting Expectations and Tips for Success

Embrace this opportunity for self-discovery with an open heart and a sense of excitement, knowing that every small victory brings you closer to a life filled with connection and fulfillment. You're not just reading a book—you're embarking on an adventure of transformation and possibility, where every challenge is met with resilience and every milestone celebrated with pride.

Take your time. There are no deadlines for any of the exercises.

Progress is gradual. Small steps lead to significant changes over time.

Practice patience. Be kind to yourself during this journey.

Flexibility is key. Adapt the book's guidance to fit your unique needs and pace.

Understanding Social Anxiety

It's time to clear up the mystery and debunk the myths surrounding this common, yet often misunderstood, condition. With this knowledge, you'll be better equipped to confront the feelings and behaviors that hold you back from living your best life.

What Is Social Anxiety?

Social anxiety is more than just shyness. It's that nagging feeling at the pit of your stomach whenever you're with a group of people; the little voice in your head constantly worrying about what others think of you. While it's normal to feel nervous or self-conscious from time to time, social anxiety takes those feelings and cranks them up to the max, making even the simplest interactions feel like climbing Mount Everest.

Anxiety is not just in our minds—our bodies feel it too. Physical reactions like sweaty palms, shaky hands, and a pounding heart all add to the intensity of the experience. But here's the thing: It's not your fault. As a human, you're hardwired to react this way, because it's your body's way of protecting you from perceived danger. It's what's often called our "fight or flight" response.

Millions of people out there—about 7 percent of the entire US population—know exactly what you're going through. Understanding that social anxiety is a common experience, not some weird personal flaw, can be a huge weight off your shoulders.

If tackling your anxiety feels too overwhelming to face on your own, seek support. Therapy can offer valuable tools and strategies to help you navigate social situations with confidence and ease, and it can help to have someone to talk and reflect with as you progress. Remember, you're stronger than you think, and you deserve to live a life filled with connection, joy, and fulfillment!

Social Anxiety and the Inner Critic

Social anxiety and the inner critic form a relentless duo, casting a shadow over social interactions and trapping us in a cycle of self-doubt. Under the harsh spotlight of your inner critic, your mind becomes a battleground where every thought and action is scrutinized and every perceived misstep is amplified. It's the voice that whispers, "They're judging you" and "You'll embarrass yourself," turning everyday encounters into overwhelming trials of scrutiny and self-critique.

Why do we have this inner critic? Evolutionarily speaking, it may have served as a survival mechanism—the same "fight or flight" instinct, for example, that told primitive humans to run from lions in the wild. However, in today's world, this survival instinct often does more harm than good. It can breed overthinking and analysis paralysis, confining us to a cycle of avoidance and withdrawal.

By acknowledging the inner critic's presence and learning to challenge its authority, we can begin to reclaim control. Techniques like cognitive restructuring and mindfulness can empower individuals to challenge negative self-talk and cultivate self-compassion. By fostering supportive inner dialogue and embracing self-acceptance, we can dismantle the power of the inner critic.

Social Anxiety and Communication

Social anxiety can seriously mess with our ability to communicate. We all know how important it is to shoot the breeze and connect with others, but when social anxiety creeps in, it's like our brain hits the panic button. Suddenly, every little interaction feels like a high-stakes game of "don't mess up."

Circling back to our inner critic—that backseat driver constantly nit-picks everything we say or do. Throw in some overthinking, and bam! We're stuck in a loop of second-guessing ourselves and worrying about what others think.

Then there are social cues, the subtle hints that help us navigate conversations and interactions with others. Social anxiety and our inner critic love to mess with those too. The negative self-talk they plant in our minds can make us wonder if a compliment is really an underhanded insult, or if a friend's smile is really an annoyed smirk.

When we doubt ourselves, we struggle to make eye contact, read the room, and engage confidently with the world around us. The fear of judgment and rejection keeps us from being fully present in the moment, because we're too preoccupied with our perceived flaws. The resulting awkward or misinterpreted interactions then reinforce our negative beliefs, further fueling the inner critic and perpetuating the cycle of anxiety.

Learning and Coping

Let's get real about social anxiety. Can it just vanish overnight? Nope, it's probably more helpful to think of it as a shadow that follows you around. Breakthroughs happen, but they're more like a slow burn than an instant fix. It's all about building trust in yourself one step at a time.

So, buckle up. The journey ahead might be a bit rocky, but with a little persistence and a whole lot of self-love, you've got what it takes to break free from social anxiety's grasp and stride confidently into a brighter tomorrow. Let's do this!

Part I

PRACTICAL SKILLS

Social anxiety can affect every aspect of life, but with the right skills, you can regain control of your day-to-day life so you're not weighed down by constant fear. The skills presented in this book might not come easy at first—they'll often challenge very engrained, sometimes even unconscious, habits. Breaking out of those patterns will require consistent practice, as though training a new muscle group. With patience, persistence, and self-compassion, you'll be able to identify and transform unhelpful thoughts and behaviors, allowing you to live a more fulfilling life and make meaningful social connections.

1
Find Your Center

In dealing with social anxiety, finding your center is
essential. Social situations can trigger overwhelming
feelings that make it difficult to stay focused and com-
posed. The skills in this chapter will help you create
a mental anchor, so you can remain grounded even in
stressful situations. As you become more adept at this,
your newfound confidence will empower you to engage
more fully in life, breaking free from the limitations of
anxiety. Remember that practice makes perfect. Think
of these mental exercises the same way you would think
of physical exercise. It takes dedication, persistence,
and repetition before you begin to see results.

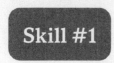
Skill #1

Centering Visualization

Social events can leave us emotionally drained and overwhelmed. This skill is a powerful tool designed to help you find your inner calm and regain equilibrium. By using your imagination, you can create a mental sanctuary where you release tension, connect deeply with your breath, and actively cultivate a profound sense of peace and resilience. This centering visualization is more than a quick fix; it's a lifelong skill. By regularly practicing this technique, you'll find it easier to stay calm, even in the most challenging situations. Remember, your inner peace is always within reach.

1. **Settle into comfort.** Find a quiet, comfortable spot where you can sit or lie down without interruptions. Close your eyes and take a few deep breaths, letting the day's stress melt away.

2. **Visualize a safe haven.** Imagine yourself in a peaceful place. It could be a lush forest, a secluded beach, or a cozy mountain cabin. Choose a place where you feel completely safe and at ease. Visualize every detail vividly.

3. **Engage your senses.** Bring your imaginary environment to life.

    -   **Sight.** Notice the vibrant colors around you.

    -   **Sound.** Listen to soothing sounds, like rustling leaves or lapping waves.

    -   **Touch.** Feel textures, such as soft sand or a cool breeze.

    -   **Smell.** Imagine the fresh scent of pine trees or salty ocean air.

    -   **Taste.** Perhaps you can taste refreshing cool water or comforting tea.

4. **Connect with your breath.** Imagine each inhale as a wave of calmness washing over you, and each exhale as a release of tension. Feel the rhythm of your breath grounding you.

5. **Release tension.** Scan your body for areas where you might feel tightness or other unpleasant sensations. With each exhale, imagine releasing this physical tension and letting it dissolve into your peaceful surroundings. Feel your body become lighter and more relaxed.

6. **Find your center.** Visualize a glowing ball of light at the center of your being, representing your inner essence and strength. See this light expanding with each breath, filling you with calm, confidence, and resilience. Let this light guide you back to your center.

7. **Return to the present.** When you feel ready, slowly bring your awareness back to the present moment. Wiggle your fingers and toes, take a few deep breaths, and open your eyes. Carry with you the sense of peace and centeredness you've cultivated, so it is within reach in difficult moments.

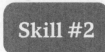
Skill #2

Active Listening

Effective communication is the cornerstone of strong personal and professional relationships. Listening skills are key if you want to communicate effectively. Active listening reduces social anxiety by helping you focus on the other person's words rather than your worries or self-doubt. By deeply engaging in what the other person is saying, you naturally shift your attention away from anxious thoughts, creating a more relaxed and confident interaction.

By fully engaging in conversation and being genuinely attentive, you demonstrate respect and empathy toward the speaker. This helps to build trust and encourages open and honest communication. Empathy eases anxiety by helping you focus on understanding others' emotions instead of dwelling on your own worries. By genuinely connecting with another person's feelings, you can reduce self-consciousness and feel more at ease during interactions.

Practice by describing a recent conversation or scenario where communication with someone felt unclear or anxiety-inducing. What was happening? What did you say to the person, or vice versa? Why do you feel there was poor communication?

_____

_____

_____

_____

_____

_____

Now let's examine this anxiety-inducing interaction to see what was going on:

VERBAL CUES List words or phrases from the speaker that caught your attention or sparked anxiety. What verbal cues did you communicate?	
NONVERBAL CUES List cues like body language or eye contact that caught your attention or sparked anxiety. What were some of your own cues?	
SHOWING EMPATHY Describe how you expressed understanding toward the other person's experience or feelings.	
ENGAGEMENT Reflect on moments when you felt like an active participant in the conversation, or showed interest in what the other person was saying.	
EMOTIONS Identify specific emotions conveyed by the speaker. Identify emotions you felt and conveyed (or tried to convey).	

UNDERLYING MESSAGES Were there messages that went unsaid, but you feel might be something the other person was "really" saying or feeling?	
QUESTIONS List ways to deepen or clarify the conversation. Did you ask questions to show that you were engaged? If so, did they impact your understanding of the situation?	
MAIN POINTS Summarize or paraphrase the speaker's main points.	
RESPONSE Reflect on the speaker's response to your active listening.	

Reflection

- What insights did you gain about your own listening habits?
- How did you feel during the conversation?
- Did you feel more connected to the person when you actively listened?
- What "listening goals" can you set for future conversations? (A "listening goal" might be fully understanding the speaker's perspective before offering your opinion.)

Skill #3

Getting to Know Your Inner Critic

Our goal is to transform anxious thoughts and behaviors, but we can't do this if we don't first observe and understand them. This exercise offers practical steps to recognize and respond to your inner critic in a way that fosters positive interactions.

1. **Identify.** Think about a recent interaction or situation where you noticed your inner critic becoming active. What triggered its appearance? What were the specific thoughts or self-judgments that arose during this interaction? Write down your reflections.

   _____

   _____

   _____

   _____

2. **Label.** Imagine that your inner critic has a persona or identity separate from yourself. Give it a name or label that represents its critical voice. Write down the name you've chosen for your inner critic.

   _____

   _____

   _____

   _____

3. **Recognize.** Write a few phrases you can tell yourself to take note that your negative thoughts have taken over. Think of them as little alarms that go off in your head when your anxiety gets triggered, so you can be more aware of your reactions.

_____

_____

_____

_____

4. **Practice in real time.** Visualize yourself in an anxiety-inducing setting where your inner critic starts to speak up. Write down the trigger phrase or cue you would use to label its voice at that moment. How would you apply this skill to acknowledge and label your inner critic as it shows up?

_____

_____

_____

_____

5. **Respond with compassion.** Reflect on how you can respond to your inner critic's critical messages with self-compassion. Write down a brief self-compassionate statement or affirmation that you could use to counteract the negativity while maintaining a sense of connection with others.

_____

_____

_____

_____

6. **Share**. Consider sharing your reflections and insights with other people facing similar challenges. Encourage open dialogue and mutual support as you explore strategies for managing the inner critic in daily life.

_____

_____

_____

_____

7. **Put your awareness into action.** Think about how you can integrate this practice into your daily interactions. What small adjustments can you make to foster a culture of self-awareness and compassion?

_____

_____

_____

_____

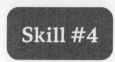

Mastering a Compassionate Mindset

Navigating social anxiety goes beyond managing symptoms. It involves changing the internal dialogue that influences your reactions. A compassionate mindset can empower you to replace self-criticism with understanding and kindness, thereby enhancing your ability to face social situations with increased confidence and calm. This approach encourages deeper self-awareness and fosters confidence in the face of social challenges.

1. **Identify triggers.** Discover what sparks your social anxiety. Is it the thought of upcoming events, habitual negative self-talk, or remnants of past experiences? Identifying these triggers is the first step toward taking control.

2. **Acknowledge feelings.** When anxiety creeps in or you catch yourself in a spiral of self-criticism, take a moment to pause. Acknowledge these feelings with gentle acceptance, noting them in your journal: "I am feeling anxious right now," or "I am being too hard on myself."

3. **Challenge negative thoughts.** Tackle negative thoughts head-on by questioning their accuracy and using kind affirmations. Write your own thoughts and responses below.

   • Negative thought: "I always mess up in social settings."

   • Compassionate response: "Everyone feels nervous sometimes. Mistakes are part of learning and growing." "I deserve compassion from myself and others." "I am capable, even in moments of anxiety."

_____

_____

_____

4. **Reflect on your practice.** After engaging in this compassionate
    self-talk routine, reflect on the changes you observe. How have
    your emotions shifted? What insights emerge from challenging
    negative thoughts? Regular reflection allows you to fine-tune
    your self-compassion practice as you move from one social inter-
    action to the next.

_____

_____

_____

5. **Share.** If comfortable, share your journey with friends or in a sup-
    port group. Discussing challenges and victories can inspire others
    and deepen your own understanding of how to navigate social
    anxiety. This isn't just about coping; it's about thriving and making
    room for more meaningful interactions with others.

A Path to Self-Forgiveness

Social anxiety can leave us wallowing in self-pity or regret after particularly uncomfortable interactions. This skill is designed to help you reduce the distress and negative self-talk that can follow such situations, by guiding you in the practice of self-forgiveness. Forgiveness cultivates emotional resilience, enabling you to approach future social situations with increased self-awareness and confidence.

1. **Prepare.** Choose a comfortable spot where you can sit or lie down undisturbed. Start with several deep breaths to relax your body and clear your mind, preparing yourself for introspection.

2. **Recall the situation.** Reflect on a recent social interaction that did not unfold as expected, leaving you feeling uneasy or anxious. Approach this memory gently, refraining from harsh self-judgment.

3. **Acknowledge your feelings.** Identify any negative thoughts or emotions that arose during and after the interaction. It's completely natural to experience these feelings. Acknowledging them without judgment is a crucial step toward changing unhealthy thoughts and behaviors.

4. **Visualize warmth and calm.** Envision a bright, comforting light encircling you. Imagine this light as a symbol of your inner calm and allow its warmth to soothe your anxieties.

5. **Ground yourself.** Take a deep breath and feel your feet firmly planted on the ground, like the roots of a sturdy tree. Allow the strength and stability of this connection to center your anxious thoughts and emotions.

6. **Affirm forgiveness.** Whisper to yourself, "I forgive myself." Recognize that everyone makes mistakes; it's a fundamental aspect of the human experience.

7. **Brighten your inner light.** With each inhale, imagine the light within growing brighter, filling you with kindness and understanding. With each exhale, release the darkness of negative thoughts.

8. **Relish the calm.** Allow yourself several moments to bask in the tranquility and comfort provided by your visualization. Let this peaceful sensation permeate every part of your body and mind, akin to warm sunlight breaking through clouds.

9. **Return to the present.** When you're ready, slowly transition back to the current moment. Take a few more deep breaths and embrace the peace you've cultivated, knowing this calm is yours to keep.

Reflection

- How did it feel to dedicate a moment to self-forgiveness?
- Did you observe any changes in your feelings toward the social situation after completing this exercise?
- What strategies can you implement to regularly remind yourself to be kind and forgiving, especially when confronting social anxiety?

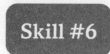

Skill #6

Ocean Breath Technique

When social anxiety strikes, our thoughts and emotions are all over the place. The ocean breath technique is designed to guide your breath—and consequently, your thoughts—into a soothing, rhythmic pattern. This method not only reduces the symptoms of anxiety in the moment; it also enhances your overall emotional equilibrium which in turn can help you navigate future situations with more calm.

1. **Find a quiet space.** Select a location where you can remain undisturbed for the duration of the exercise. Ideal spots might include a rarely used conference room, a quiet corner of a library, or a peaceful outdoor area.

2. **Get comfortable.** Settle into a comfortable position that supports relaxation. This could be sitting cross-legged on a cushion, reclining in a comfy chair, or lying down on a yoga mat. Ensure that your posture allows for deep breathing.

3. **Understand the technique.** Familiarize yourself with the breathing pattern and counting sequence involved. Having a sense of the flow beforehand will reduce distractions and increase the effectiveness of the skill.

4. **Practice the pattern.** Begin the breathing sequence, aiming to complete five full cycles to fully experience its benefits:

   • **Inhale.** Gently inhale through your nose, counting slowly to four, making sure your lungs are fully expanded, drawing calmness into your body.

- **Hold.** Pause with the air inside for another slow count of four, absorbing the stillness and fullness that it brings to every part of your body.

- **Exhale.** Gradually release the breath through your mouth, counting slowly to four, actively expelling all the air and with it, the built-up stress and tension.

- **Hold.** After fully exhaling, hold your breath for a count of four, embracing the quiet emptiness and peace this brings.

- **Repeat.w** Continue this breathing pattern, concentrating on maintaining a steady rhythm and allowing the calming effects to deepen with each cycle.

Reflection

- How did practicing the ocean breath technique make you feel?
- Did you notice any physical or mental changes during the exercise?
- How can you integrate this technique into your daily routine? Is there a regular time or place where you can pause to breathe?
- How might regular practice of this technique impact your reactions in stressful social situations?

Skill #7

Finding Calm Through Hobbies

Hobbies offer a sense of fulfillment and social connection that helps reduce anxiety and isolation. When these activities are shared with others, they also offer a controlled environment for exploring inter-actions and relationships. Here we'll explore how you can make pleasant hobbies a consistent part of your anti-anxiety routine.

Morning reflection (5 minutes): Begin each day by choosing an activity that might help you feel more prepared for challenging situa-tions or interactions you anticipate. Whether it's something soothing like sketching, or more active like participating in a book club, jot down your intentions for engaging in this hobby today.

Midday hobby break (15–30 minutes): Schedule a midday break dedicated to your chosen hobby. This isn't just about filling time; it's about intentionally engaging in an activity that boosts your mood and confidence. If your hobby involves others, like a virtual game or a discussion group, see it as an opportunity to practice skills such as active listening in a low-stress setting. Record any feelings of anxiety and how the hobby helps manage them.

Evening wind-down (20 minutes): End your day with an activity that helps you decompress and reflect on your social interactions, like journaling or meditation. This reflection is crucial for reinforcing posi-tive social experiences or learning from challenging ones.

Weekly exploration (1 hour per week): Once a week, dedicate time to explore a new hobby or sharpen a skill you've been working on. This keeps your routine exciting and keeps "hobby time" from becoming another mundane task. Document what you tried, what you learned, and whether it's something you'd like to incorporate more regularly.

Mindful engagement: While engaged in your hobbies, practice mindfulness. Focus deeply on the task at hand—observe the colors in your painting, feel the soil in your hands, or listen to the sound of the piano keys. This practice anchors you in the present moment, allowing us to release the past or future moments of anxiety.

Gratitude log (5 minutes before bed): Write down three things from your daily hobby session that you appreciate. Perhaps you're grateful for the peace you felt while drawing, or for the excitement of learning a new guitar chord. This not only ends your day on a positive note but also reinforces the benefits of your hobbies.

Reflection

- As you integrate these pleasant activities into your daily life, think about how they change your approach to stress and overall happiness.
- How can you further enhance the benefits of this practice?

Skill #8

Bias Buster

Social anxiety is driven by negative beliefs about ourselves and others—we fear that a love interest thinks we're ugly, or that we're too boring to make new friends. In this way, we are approaching life with unhelpful biases. As paralyzing as they can be, these biases are often based on our own unfounded assumptions. Cognitive-behavioral therapy refers to these biases as "cognitive distortions" because they distort how we understand the world. The following skill encourages you to shift your perspective so that you can make room for more meaningful connections.

1. **Identify your assumptions.** Consider an interaction or situation that causes you social anxiety. Now dig deeper into the thinking behind your discomfort:

   - What specific belief are you holding about this social situation? If this is hard to pinpoint, think about what your inner critic (or whatever label you've given your anxiety) is telling you.

   - Where did this belief originate? Is it rooted in real experiences or unfounded assumptions?

   - How has this belief influenced your behavior in past social interactions?

   _____

   _____

   _____

2. **Challenge the evidence.** Play detective with your own thoughts. Assess the evidence supporting your assumptions to test their validity:

- What concrete evidence do I have that supports this belief?

- Can you remember instances where this belief was proven wrong?

- Are you focusing only on details that support your bias, and ignoring those that contradict it?

_____

_____

_____

_____

3. **Explore alternative perspectives.** Open your mind to new viewpoints that can help soften rigid thought patterns:

- What are some other ways to interpret this situation?

- How might someone with a different perspective view this same scenario?

- What positive outcomes could arise that you haven't considered?

_____

_____

_____

_____

4. **Consider the consequences.** Think about the impact of sticking with these biases:

- How do these beliefs affect your emotions and behavior in social settings?

- How will maintaining these assumptions affect your relationships and mental health in the long term?

- What might change for the better if you altered your perspective?

_____

_____

_____

_____

5. **Challenge logical fallacies.** Identify and challenge cognitive distortions that skew your reasoning. Here are some common traps you could be caught in:

- Engaging in black-and-white thinking that keeps you from seeing nuance

- Overgeneralizing from a few experiences

- Catastrophizing the situation by seeing only the worst possible outcome

_____

_____

_____

_____

6. **Seek resolution.** Reflect on what you've uncovered to find ways to adjust your mindset:

- What new insights have you gained about your social fears?

- How can you use this new understanding to approach social situations more confidently?

- What specific steps can you take to challenge and change your biases in future interactions?

_____

_____

_____

_____

2
Stop Overthinking

Overthinking can turn social situations into a mental obstacle course. But don't worry—these skills are your superhero toolkit! Before a stressful event, they help you suit up with confidence and clarity. During the event, they keep you grounded and present, making conversations more relaxed. Afterward, they help you look back on the event through a positive lens, avoiding an endless replay loop. By quieting the self-doubt that comes with overthinking, you can more confidently step into stressful situations.

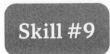

Observe and Release

Imagine navigating through a busy day when, suddenly, your mind starts to race with a flood of thoughts—worries, what-ifs, and doubts. It's like being caught in a mental whirlwind. But instead of getting swept away, you have a secret technique to observe these thoughts, let them pass, and find calm in the storm. This approach is rooted in mindfulness, helping you notice your thoughts without becoming overwhelmed.

1. **Find your focus.** Begin by finding a comfortable spot where you can sit quietly. Like in the previous breathing exercise, take a few deep breaths to settle your mind and body.

2. **Shift to observation.** As you breathe calmly, gently shift your attention to your thoughts. Notice what comes to mind—whether it's a worry, a memory, or a random thought. Observe it without trying to judge or change it.

3. **Label and release.** When a thought arises, mentally label it (e.g., "worry," "planning," "doubt"). After labeling it, imagine it as a cloud drifting by in the sky. Watch it pass without getting caught up, knowing that thoughts are temporary and you don't need to control your emotions or actions.

4. **Practice non-attachment.** If you're getting pulled into a thought, gently remind yourself to let it go. Bring your focus back to your breathing, using it as an anchor to stay grounded in the present moment.

5. **Return to the present.** After a few minutes of observing and releasing your thoughts, bring your attention fully back to your surroundings. Notice the sights, sounds, and sensations around you. Ground yourself in the present moment, free from the hold of overthinking.

6. **Affirm your calm.** Could you conclude the exercise by confirming your ability to manage overthinking? Quietly say to yourself, "I can observe my thoughts without being controlled by them. I am present and at peace."

7. **Carry the calm forward.** As you return to your day, carry this sense of calm and mindfulness. Know that you can return to this practice to regain control when overthinking starts to take over.

Reflection

- How did observing your thoughts without getting caught up in them feel?
- Did you notice any difference in how you responded to your thoughts after this exercise?
- How can you incorporate this practice into your everyday life?

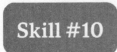

Skill #10

Reframing Anxious Thoughts

Social anxiety can make interactions feel like a maze of negative thoughts and overthinking. Once you get trapped in them, it can be hard to break free and it's easy to feel like you're no longer in control. Reframing helps you flip those thoughts around and see things in a more balanced and positive light. Imagine transforming your anxiety into a superpower, helping you stay calm and confident in any social setting. Once you're able to stop negative thoughts in their tracks, you can begin to break the bad habit of overthinking.

Think of a situation that triggered your social anxiety and identify the negative thoughts that came up for you. What was your inner critic telling you in that moment? Once you've pinpointed a few of those thoughts, keep them in mind as you go through the following steps:

Reflection

- How did it feel to challenge and reframe your negative thoughts?
- Did reframing negative thoughts help to quiet your overthinking mind?
- Did you notice any changes in your anxiety levels during social interactions when you applied this skill?
- How can you incorporate these techniques into your daily routine to maintain a balanced perspective and reduce social anxiety?

EVALUATE	REFRAME	
1. **Question the evidence**	What evidence do I have that this thought is true? Is there another way to interpret this situation?	
2. **Consider alternative perspectives**	Could people be preoccupied with their own concerns instead of judging me?	
3. **Challenge catastrophic thinking**	What's the worst that could realistically happen? How likely is it that this outcome will occur?	
4. **Generate counter-arguments**	Have there been times when I handled similar situations well?	

EVALUATE	REFRAME	
5. Practice positive self-talk	What positive statements can I use to replace my negative thoughts? Examples: "I am capable," "I am likable," "I can handle social situations with ease."	
6. Visualize success	How can I visualize myself succeeding in social interactions?	
7. Practice mindfulness	What mindfulness techniques can I use to stay present during social interactions?	
8. Celebrate progress	What progress have I made in challenging negative thoughts and reducing social anxiety? How can I continue to use these techniques to maintain a balanced perspective?	

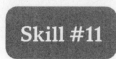

Reality Check: Don't Believe Everything You Think

Social anxiety can often lead to "mind reading," where you assume you know what others are thinking, which in turn fuels your own negative thoughts. The interesting thing is that thoughts are just that—thoughts! No matter how powerful, they are not necessarily accurate or correct. This skill helps loosen the grip that these negative assumptions have on the way you interact with others.

1. **Notice when you're mind reading.** Take note of when you start guessing what others are thinking about you. When do you catch yourself guessing what others think about you? Is it during conversations, in a group, or when you're alone?

   _____

   _____

   _____

2. **Question your assumptions.** Ask yourself if there's any real evidence for what you're thinking. Are you jumping to conclusions without any proof? If not, what proof supports your assumptions? Remember that thoughts are just thoughts and not necessarily true.

   _____

   _____

   _____

3. **Consider alternative explanations.** Think about other reasons why someone might act a certain way. What else could explain someone's behavior? For example, could they be having a bad day or be distracted by something else?

_____

_____

_____

_____

4. **Focus on facts.** Stick to what you know for sure. What facts do you know about the situation? If you're unsure, would it be better to ask directly than to assume? How might you clarify the situation?

_____

_____

_____

_____

5. **Center your thoughts.** Replace negative thoughts with more balanced ones. Instead of assuming the worst, can you think, "I don't know what they're thinking, but it's okay because I'm doing my best"? What else could you tell yourself in this situation?

_____

_____

_____

6. **Practice self-compassion.** Be kind to yourself and remember everyone makes mistakes. How can you show kindness to yourself? Can you remind yourself that it's normal to feel anxious, but it doesn't mean your thoughts are always accurate?

_____

_____

_____

_____

Reflection

- How did it feel to question and challenge your "mind reading"?
- After applying the skill, did you notice any changes in your anxiety levels during social interactions?
- How can you incorporate these techniques into your daily routine to keep overthinking at bay?

Event Reflection Ritual

Social events like parties or conferences stir up all kinds of anxious feelings. When anxiety strikes, self-reflection can help us pause long enough to gain insight into our thoughts and behavior, making the way for personal growth. This skill will help you incorporate this moment of pause into your everyday life by making a ritual of it, allowing you to re-center and decompress from these events. It can also help you counter the overthinking and rumination that often follows uncomfortable interactions.

Use the following steps and prompts after a social event—this can be a conversation, a party, a date—to reflect and re-center with self-compassion.

1. **Settle into the moment.** Find a calm spot free from distractions, and set a calming mood by lighting a candle or playing soft music. Take a few deep breaths to center yourself. Close your eyes and let go of immediate stress or distractions.

2. **Recall the event.** Think about the venue, the people you engaged with, and the conversations that took place. Write down your thoughts and emotions as they come to you. Be as detailed as possible.

_____

_____

_____

_____

3. **Highlight the positives.** Write down any moments of joy, connection, or achievement. Recognize and celebrate these successes.

_____

_____

_____

_____

4. **Face the challenges.** Write down the moments when you felt uncomfortable or anxious. Note any patterns in your thoughts or behaviors, or in what triggered your discomfort. Recognize these challenges as opportunities for growth.

_____

_____

_____

_____

5. **Gain insights.** What did you learn about yourself during the event? What strengths did you show? What areas do you want to improve for future interactions?

_____

_____

_____

_____

6. **Challenge negative thoughts.** Consider the repetitive thought patterns or negative rumination you've identified. Practice self-compassion and bring your focus back to the present moment. Jot down some of these negative thoughts to release their power.

_____

_____

_____

_____

7. **Set goals.** Write down specific actions or skills to work on for future social interactions. Outline short-term steps that will move you toward these goals.

_____

_____

_____

_____

8. **Express gratitude.** Write a few sentences of gratitude, appreciating the positives from the social event.

_____

_____

_____

Flip the Script

Flipping the script is about reversing self-rejection. This approach shifts your focus from negative actions to positive ones, enhancing your confidence and well-being. Follow the steps to examine your own actions and record your findings in the blank spaces.

STEP	ACTION	
Spot negative behaviors	Notice when you're undermining your self-worth. Example: Realizing you're avoiding social events because you feel inadequate.	
Pause and acknowledge	Recognize that these actions aren't serving you. Example: Admitting that avoiding events is making you feel more isolated.	

Challenge negative thoughts	Counter negative thoughts with kind and realistic statements. Example: Replacing "I can't do this" with "I can handle small steps."	
Commit to opposite action	Choose to do something positive, even if it feels uncomfortable. Example: Joining a small social gathering or spending time on a hobby you love.	
Notice the difference	Pay attention to how you feel after taking the positive action. Example: Feeling more connected and positive after the meetup.	

CLEAR

As the name suggests, this skill helps you clear away thoughts that do not serve you. It's an easy-to-remember acronym that can guide you through the process of challenging, learning, evaluating, adjusting, and reframing as you face your anxiety head-on.

CHALLENGE. Often, our mind leaps to extremes, but reality is more nuanced. Challenging these thoughts opens a door to a more balanced view. Notice overgeneralized thoughts like "I always mess up in social situations" and ask yourself if it's true that this is *always* the case.

LEARN. Pay attention to when these thoughts pop up, and observe how they make you feel. Consider the origins of these thoughts. Are they remnants of past experiences? Identify triggers or behavior patterns. By becoming familiar with them, you gain insight into their hold on you.

EVALUATE. Think about whether there's any evidence to support these thoughts. Consider alternative perspectives that could counter these thoughts. Evaluating these thoughts against reality can dismantle their influence.

ADJUST. Shift your perspective if the thought isn't entirely true. Doing this can empower you to take control over your own narrative. Allow yourself to consider alternatives.

REFRAME. Take one of your overwhelming thoughts or ruminations, and reword it so that it is not as extreme. For example, change "I always mess up" to "Sometimes things don't go as planned, but I've also had successful interactions." This helps you transform failure to resilience, highlighting your ability to navigate challenges successfully.

Creative Thought Tracker

This skill helps you manage overthinking by visualizing and expressing your thoughts and emotions in creative ways. By treating your overthinking as an artistic adventure, you can gain new insights and find enjoyable ways to redirect your mind. Engaging in creative activities can also significantly reduce stress by offering moments of relaxation. Feel free to write or draw—whichever form of expression is calling you that day.

Set the scene: Depict the event or interaction that triggered your overthinking. Include vivid details, colors, smells, words that were said.

> *Example: "I started overthinking after my friend didn't reply to my message right away."*

Imagination voyage: Visualize your overthinking as a scene from a book or movie. Describe or draw it in simple, inventive terms.

Example: A sketch of a stormy sea with huge waves crashing over a boat.

Feelings sketch: Draw or describe your emotions in a creative way. Use simple doodles or metaphors to express how you felt.

Example: "I felt like a balloon being blown up, ready to burst."

Intensity scale: Consider a scale that goes from "calm" to "chaotic." Use simple labels or images to describe how strong your overthinking felt.

Example: A sketch of a person cowering in fear of a huge dragon, to represent how you feel when you're overwhelmed with negative thoughts.

Mind tree: Identify recurring thoughts and sketch them out like branches on a tree. Keep it simple and visual.

Main thought: "My friend is ignoring me."
- Branch—"They must be upset with me."
- Branch—"I did something wrong."

Challenge adventure: Imagine your fight against social anxiety as a hero's quest. Depict or describe what it looks like to conquer this enemy.

Example: "I imagine myself as a knight facing a dragon of doubt and slaying it with a sword of reassurance."

Outcome sketch: Draw or describe how this particular moment of your overthinking ended. What happened after you slayed your anxiety dragon?

Example: "After taking a walk, I felt calmer and realized the friend who canceled on me might just be busy. I was able to let it go and enjoy the rest of the day."

Insights: Draw or write down any creative ideas or insights you gained from these exercises.

Example: A person swimming against the riptide, to depict the insight that sometimes your overthinking only makes the situation worse.

Flex Your Mind

Social anxiety traps us in a loop of fear and regret. We fear future interactions, and regret past ones. Think of this skill as a mental workout—one that helps you build up muscle to break free from those pesky "should" thoughts, and from the inner critic that expects you to be perfect. Research shows that being more flexible and open-minded in our thinking can lower anxiety and depression. If you're tired of overthinking, this method can be a game-changer by helping you break free from negative thought loops to embrace a more positive, resilient mindset.

1. **Notice the "should" thoughts.** Pay attention to thoughts that include words like "should," "ought to," or "must." These are often rigid and demanding, and they're a signal that you're stuck in the past.

2. **Ask yourself: Is this realistic?** Question whether the "should" thought is realistic and fair. Consider if there are other ways to look at the situation.

3. **Change the thought.** Replace the demanding thought with a more flexible one. For example, change "I must always be perfect" to "It's okay to make mistakes; they help me learn."

4. **Be kind to yourself.** "Should" thoughts can be very unkind and impatient with us. Take a moment to treat yourself with kindness and remind yourself that it's okay to have flaws and limitations.

5. **Set achievable goals.** Set goals that are realistic and achievable. Focus on progress, not perfection. Celebrate your successes, no matter how small.

6. **Practice, practice, practice!** Keep practicing changing your "should" thoughts. The more you do it, the easier it becomes to be kinder to yourself and see things from a more balanced perspective.

3
(How To) Talk to People

Talking to people can be challenging, especially when social situations feel daunting. Mental preparation and staying present during interactions can make a big difference. In this chapter you'll learn critical communication skills like making eye contact, using open body language, and asking engaging questions to enhance your conversations. With regular practice, these skills will transform your ability to create meaningful connections with other people.

Blueprint for Assertive Communication

This blueprint empowers you to express needs and boundaries so you can engage more positively in social settings and cultivate healthier relationships. Confident and assertive communication can ultimately help prevent misunderstandings that lead to stressful conflict.

1. **Describe the situation.** Clearly describe the interaction needing assertive communication. Stick to the facts, avoiding assumptions.

    Example: "During our meetings, I've noticed that discussions sometimes move forward before everyone has had the chance to contribute." Reflect on how the dominant member's actions impact the group dynamics and the feelings of other members.

    _____

    _____

    _____

    _____

    _____

    _____

2. **Express your feelings.** Use "I" statements to share your feelings about the situation. Be precise and honest about your emotional response.

Example: "I feel overlooked when we proceed without hearing everyone's input, as it makes me feel my contributions are under-valued." Acknowledge your feelings of frustration and concern about the inclusiveness of the meetings.

_____

_____

_____

_____

_____

3. **Assert.** State your needs clearly and precisely. Describe what changes you expect.

   Example: Specify the need for a more structured approach to discussions that allows equal opportunity for input. "I would appreciate it if we could ensure everyone has a chance to speak before making decisions."

_____

_____

_____

_____

_____

4. **Support with evidence.** Provide examples or factual information that supports your perspective.

   Example: Cite specific instances where valuable contributions were missed due to the current dynamics. "In the last few meetings, we skipped over feedback from newer members, which could lead to missed insights."

_____

_____

_____

_____

5. **Attention to nonverbal cues.** Monitor your body language and tone to ensure they convey assertiveness, not aggression.

   Example: Maintain eye contact with community members. When you speak, use a calm tone even if you're feeling agitated. Check that your body language is positive—don't cross your arms or look distracted if other people join in.

6. **Project confidence.** Prepare yourself before speaking, so you're clear about what you're trying to communicate.

   Example: Before speaking, you make a list of all the points you want to make. During the break, you go to your car for five minutes to rehearse what you're going to say, taking notes so you have a loose script.

_____

_____

_____

_____

_____

7. **Negotiate and collaborate.** Invite feedback and be open to discussion. Aim for a solution that respects both your needs and those of others.

   Example: Once you're done, turn the conversation back to the group. "What do you guys think about implementing a structured turn-taking system during our meetings?" Encourage participation from others so you can find solutions that work for everyone.

   _____

   _____

   _____

   _____

   _____

8. **Self-validation.** Reaffirm the validity of your feelings and rights to assertive communication, regardless of the response.

   Example: "My needs are important, and expressing them respectfully is healthy and necessary." "Other people nodded in agreement, so I'm not the only one who feels this way."

   _____

   _____

   _____

   _____

   _____

SPARK

Meeting new people can be terrifying. SPARK is your ultimate method for sparking lively and meaningful conversations with people you don't know well. This approach integrates shared interests, personal anecdotes, and thoughtful questions enriched with humor and empathy to create memorable interactions. By focusing on these critical elements, SPARK helps ease the anxiety of meeting new people and provides a clear framework for building rapport.

SHARED INTERESTS. Kick off conversations by discovering mutual interests—books, music, or movies.

Example: "Love that band on your shirt! Seen them live?"

PERSONAL EXPERIENCES. Deepen the connection by swapping stories or experiences related to your interests.

Example: "I met the drummer last year at a gig. How about you? Any cool fan moments?"

ASK OPEN-ENDED QUESTIONS. Use questions that open doors to longer, more thoughtful responses.

Example: "What's one book you think everyone should read?"

REFLECTIVE LISTENING. Show your engagement by mirroring their thoughts or feelings and adding insights.

Example: "Sounds like that trip was a game-changer for you."

KINDNESS AND HUMOR. Weave in compliments and light-hearted jokes to keep the mood upbeat and inclusive.

Example: "That's an epic story! My adventures seem tame in comparison."

Power Posing

Research shows that adopting powerful poses can boost your confidence. One Harvard Business School study discovered that just two minutes of high-power posing can increase your feelings of power by a whopping 33 percent. Imagine feeling that surge of confidence every day! This skill will help you tap into that power, so get ready to strike a pose and transform your social game. Spend a few minutes each day practicing these poses before important meetings, presentations, or social events.

Mountain pose: Stand with your feet shoulder-width apart. Keep your spine straight, and imagine a string pulling you upward from the top of your head, elongating your spine, and lifting your chest. Let your hands rest at your side, and imagine you are strong and tall like a mountain.

Open posture: Uncross your arms and legs to open up your body. Keep your arms relaxed by your sides, or place your hands on your hips with your elbows pointed outward, creating a wide stance.

Wide stance: Take up space by widening your stance and occupying more physical space. Plant your feet firmly on the ground and distribute your weight evenly between both legs.

Expansive expressions: While you're speaking, let yourself gesture freely with your hands to express your thoughts. Let yourself feel confident in your own body by not crossing your arms or hunching over.

Head held high: Keep your chin parallel to the ground and your gaze looking straight ahead. Avoid tilting your head downward, which can convey submission or insecurity.

Steady eye contact: Practice making eye contact with others in a friendly and confident manner. Maintain a relaxed gaze and avoid staring or looking away too quickly.

Smile: Wear a genuine smile to radiate warmth and approachability. Smiling can help you feel more positive and relaxed, inviting others to engage with you. Practice smiling even when there's no one around, just to lift your own mood.

Breathe deeply: Take slow, deep breaths to calm your nervous system and center yourself. Inhale deeply through your nose, allowing your abdomen to expand, and exhale slowly through your mouth, releasing tension and stress.

Visualize your power: While holding a power pose, visualize yourself succeeding and achieving your goals confidently and efficiently. Picture yourself engaging confidently in social interactions and achieving positive outcomes.

Reflect on your progress: Take note of how (or if) the poses you tried out helped ease your anxiety. Might any of these help you mentally prepare for upcoming situations or interactions?

_____

_____

_____

_____

_____

_____

_____

Catch the VIBE

This approach will help you unlock the mysteries of social dynamics by honing in on visual cues, mood indicators, body language, and engagement levels. Research indicates that those who can effectively interpret social cues experience less social anxiety, transforming social interactions from nerve-wracking to effortlessly engaging. The next time you awkwardly enter a room with no idea how to engage, use the VIBE acronym to help you navigate the scene.

VISUAL SCAN. Start by visually scanning the room. Take note of the room's layout and the positioning of people. Observe where groups are forming and the overall setting. For example, notice if people gather around the snack table, sit in small groups, or mingle near the entrance. To make it more engaging, pretend it's a game. See how quickly you can spot the friendliest-looking group or the most animated conversation.

INDICATORS OF MOOD. Pay attention to the general mood and energy of the room. Listen to the noise level and watch for signs of people's feelings—happy, relaxed, serious, or tense. Are people laughing and chatting animatedly or more subdued and quietly engaged? Try to match your mood to the room's. If it's lively, allow yourself to feel more energetic; if it's calm, embrace the tranquility.

BODY LANGUAGE. Observe body language to gauge openness and engagement. Look for uncrossed arms, open stances, eye contact, and facial expressions. Are people leaning in toward each other and making eye contact, or are they turned away and avoiding interaction? Mimic the positive body language you see. If someone looks relaxed and open, adopt a similar posture.

ENGAGEMENT LEVELS. Assess people's involvement in their conversations or activities. High engagement suggests interest and activity, while low engagement might indicate boredom or disinterest. For example, are people deeply engrossed in conversation or look around the room and check their phones frequently?

How to Practice VIBE

Start small. Begin practicing in smaller settings, such as family gatherings or casual hangouts with friends.

Observe without judging. Watch what happens without rushing to make judgments or assumptions about people's intentions or feelings.

Reflect on observations. After the event, reflect on your observations. Did you accurately read the room's vibe? How did your observations make you feel?

Compare and learn. Compare your initial impressions with what later happened. Were the people you thought were open and friendly that way?

Eye See You

For many people, a lack of eye contact can convey lack of confidence or trust. This skill transforms the fear or uncertainty of making eye contact into a series of fun challenges. On this quest, each challenge brings you closer to navigating social interactions with confidence. You can do most of these in front of a mirror to start off, but for full effect, recruit friends or family to join you on this adventure!

Mirror magic: Stand in front of a mirror. While maintaining eye contact with your reflection, give yourself an animated pep talk. Hold eye contact for as long as possible while pumping yourself up for the day ahead.

Friendship face-off: Choose a friend or family member to join your eye-contact adventure. Sit facing each other and take turns making silly faces while maintaining eye contact. See who can keep a straight face the longest!

Triangle trick: Imagine you're a detective solving a mystery. Have a friend or family member pose as your "suspect." As you interrogate them, practice eye contact by focusing on the triangle between their eyes and nose. Maintain your detective composure while interrogating these "suspects."

Balance banter: With a friend, pretend you're having a conversation while walking toward each other on a balance beam. Maintain eye contact while keeping your balance. Engage actively with the conversation without losing your focus or footing.

Cultural connection quest: Research different cultures' attitudes toward eye contact. Choose one that you find particularly interesting, and practice adapting your gaze accordingly. Create a "passport" to track your quest and collect stamps from friends as you adjust your eye-contact skills.

Reflection rave: Celebrate your progress with a reflection rave! Put on your favorite song, dance around, and give yourself a high-five in the mirror while maintaining eye contact. Enjoy the fun and recognize your improvement. Let yourself decompress!

Repeat and level up: With each completed challenge, give yourself a point or treat. In order to keep improving, set new eye-contact challenges and quests for yourself. Celebrate each victory along this journey.

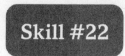

When to Stop Talking

Effective communication is about balance. Knowing when to stop talking is key to maintaining engaging and respectful conversations. A study conducted by the University of Texas showed that 55 percent of communication is body language, 38 percent is tone of voice, and only 7 percent is spoken words. This skill helps you assess the right moments to pause or end a conversation by observing body language, listening for verbal cues, and evaluating the context.

While engaging in conversation, consider the following as you speak:

1. Listener's body language:

    • Are they making eye contact and nodding?
      Yes / No

    • Are they leaning in or facing toward you?
      Yes / No

    • Do they seem distracted, or are they looking around?
      Yes / No

2. Verbal cues:

    • Are they asking questions and showing interest?
      Yes / No

    • Are their responses becoming shorter or more neutral?
      Yes / No

    • Have they mentioned needing to go or do something else?
      Yes / No

3. Reflect on the conversation balance:

    - Have you been speaking for a long time without giving them a chance to speak?
      Yes / No

    - Have you asked them questions about themselves?
      Yes / No

    - Do you feel like the conversation is turning into a monologue?
      Yes / No

4. Assess the context:

    - Is the setting appropriate for a long conversation?
      Yes / No

    - Are you aware of their time constraints or other commitments?
      Yes / No

    - Is there a natural pause or ending point in the conversation?
      Yes / No

5. Redirect the conversation:

    - If you answered "no" to several questions above, pause and ask the other person a question about themselves to re-engage them. Acknowledge the time and wrap up the conversation if needed:

      "I've been talking a lot about myself. How about you? What's new with you?"

      "I just realized I've been chatting for a while. Don't want to keep you if you need to go!"

Daily Check-In

You can uncover valuable insights into your social anxiety, and how to best cope with it, by taking just a few moments each day to reflect on conversations and interactions. This skill is like a personal growth adventure—track your progress, identify improvement areas, and boost your confidence. Consistent self-reflection is essential for mastering social interactions and making room for personal growth.

Rate each statement below based on how you felt today, using a scale from 1 to 5:

1. Not at all: I did not feel this way today.

2. Slightly: I felt this way a little bit today.

3. Somewhat: I felt this way moderately today.

4. Quite a bit: I felt this way considerably today.

5. Very much: I felt this way intensely today.

Tips

Reflect on observations: Review your ratings at the end of the week to identify any patterns or recurring challenges. Remember that these aren't grades on a test—the numbers are just a way for you to evaluate the level of your social anxiety.

Set goals: Based on your observations, set small, achievable goals to work on specific areas.

Track progress: Continue using this check-in tool daily and note any improvements or changes in your feelings over time.

OBSERVATION	RATING
I felt anxious or nervous when initiating a conversation with someone I didn't know well.	
I worried about what they thought of me while talking to them.	
I avoided social situations or talking to others because I feared embarrassment or rejection.	
I struggled to maintain eye contact during conversations.	
I found it challenging to think of things to say in social situations.	
I felt self-conscious or judged when speaking in front of others.	
I often rehearsed or overthought what I would say before speaking to someone.	
I experienced physical symptoms of anxiety (e.g. sweating, trembling, rapid heartbeat) when talking to others.	
I frequently compared myself to others in social situations.	
I worried about saying something embarrassing or making a mistake when talking to others.	
I found speaking up or asserting myself in group settings challenging.	
I often felt like I didn't belong or fit in when interacting with others.	
I felt relieved when social interactions ended or when I could leave a conversation.	
I avoided making phone or video calls because of anxiety about talking to others.	

PAUSE

The PAUSE skill is your go-to strategy for wrapping up conversations smoothly and without any awkwardness. Think of it as a fun and friendly way to keep interactions positive while giving yourself an easy out when needed. Knowing how to do this can rapidly reduce your anxiety as you manage social interactions. So, let's make ending conversations as enjoyable as starting them!

The next time you're feeling awkward or uncomfortable in a conversation, use the PAUSE acronym to remember ways to confidently end the interaction.

POLITELY INTERRUPT

- Gently insert a pause into the conversation.
  Example: "Sorry to interrupt, but ..."

ACKNOWLEDGE THE INTERACTION

- Show Appreciation for the Conversation.
  Example: "I've enjoyed our chat."

USE AN EXCUSE

- Provide a reason for needing to leave.
  Example: "I need to catch up with someone else," or "I have to make a call."

SUGGEST FUTURE CONTACT

- Offer to reconnect at a later time.
  Example: "Let's catch up again soon," or "We should talk more later."

EXIT GRACEFULLY

- End with a polite gesture and farewell.
  Example: "Take care!" or "See you later!"

Part II

NAVIGATING SOCIAL SITUATIONS

N ow we move into Part II, where I'll help you navigate everyday social situations that leave you feeling stuck or panicked.

Together, we'll dive into relatable, real-life scenarios and explore what's happening in each one. You'll gain insights into why certain situations trigger anxiety and learn practical steps to handle them.

Using the skills from Part I, I'll guide you through step-by-step exercises designed to build confidence. With dedication and practice, these skills can help you not only manage anxiety in stressful social situations, but also gain a deeper understanding of why and how your anxiety manifests—an awareness that is key in loosening anxiety's grip.

4
Friends and Acquaintances

Meeting new friends and building connections with acquaintances can feel intimidating when insecurity and social anxiety come into play. The fear of being judged, the worry of saying the wrong thing, or the pressure to "be interesting" can easily leave you feeling overwhelmed. But what if you could apply the same anxiety-management tools to these everyday social situations? In this chapter, you'll explore how to engage in conversations with ease and form genuine bonds without the constant fear of missteps. Get ready to unlock strategies that will empower you to navigate the social landscape with confidence, opening doors to rewarding, lasting friendships.

Public Embarrassment

You're at a party where you don't know many people. As guests arrive, you start to feel anxious. Your heart races and your chest tightens. The unfamiliar faces make you feel out of place. You're afraid to start a conversation, so you stay in the corner of the room and avoid eye contact. The more you think about how anxious you feel, the more anxious you get, making it virtually impossible to enjoy the party. Trapped in your own overthinking, you're left feeling isolated even in a roomful of people.

WHAT IS GOING ON

When your mind is racing with anxious thoughts, your body responds with physical symptoms of distress, which in turn only make you more nervous. Your anxiety is telling you that there's danger ahead—in this case, the potential for public embarrassment or rejection—so it triggers that primitive "fight or flight" instinct. It's important to recognize when and why this happens, so you can take steps to calm both your body and mind. The goal is to quiet the anxious thoughts and sensations just enough to rejoin the party.

ADDRESS THE ISSUE

Use Skill #9, "Observe and Release" (pp. 38–39).

1. **Find a quiet place where you can have a few minutes to yourself.** You can go take a walk, sit in your car, or even lock yourself in the bathroom if there's no other option. Once you find a comfortable spot, take a few deep breaths to find your focus.

2. **Shift to observation.** As you breathe, take note of the thoughts running through your head. Don't judge them! Just watch them as though you're a birdwatcher looking up at the sky and taking notes.

3. **Label and release.** As a thought arises, give it a name. You assign it a category, like "self-doubt," or name the thought itself, like "I'm ugly." The point is to give it a form so you can gain some control over it. Don't chase the thought, though. Just acknowledge each thought, wait for it to pass, observe the next one as it arises, and repeat the process as you continue to breathe calmly.

4. **Practice non-attachment.** When you notice yourself chasing the thought, take note of its power over you. It might be a very familiar thought that feels like factual truth, but gently remind yourself that it's just a thought—a cloud in the sky. If you find yourself slipping back into rumination again, take note of the thought that took over, and gently bring yourself back by refocusing on your breath.

5. **Return to the present.** Once the overthinking has settled, reconnect with your surroundings. One way to do this is to take note of three objects you can see (for example, floor pattern or wall color). Listen for two things you can hear (distant laughter, hum of conversation). Touch one thing within reach (your hand on cold porcelain). Tell yourself, "I'm here, in this moment. I am present." Come back to the party.

6. **Affirm your calm.** Take a final deep breath. "I feel calm and ready." Walk back to the party with peace and purpose. Rejoin your friends confidently.

Reflection

After the event, take time to assess your response, and what you learned from the experience.

- Was it difficult to observe your thoughts without chasing them?
- Did labeling your thoughts make them more or less overwhelming?
- By labeling them, were you able to recognize patterns? Were there certain thoughts that kept repeating over and over?
- How can you incorporate this mindfulness practice into your daily routine as a way of coping with negative thoughts?
- Can you develop a strategy for scanning the room and identifying a "sanctuary" when you first walk in?

Building Community

Your neighborhood association is hosting a block party. While you've interacted with some neighbors regularly in the past, others are just acquaintances you've met in passing, or complete strangers you haven't even seen before. The event is bustling with activity—kids playing games, adults chatting and laughing, and a barbecue filling the air with mouth-watering smells. You want to make the most of this opportunity to build stronger relationships within your community. However, you dread striking up conversations because you worry about awkward silences, or coming across as insincere. You worry the neighbors will think you're weird, or that they'll talk about you behind your back the next day. You step out for a few minutes, but quickly go back home because the packed block is too intimidating.

WHAT IS GOING ON

Social anxiety can leave you feeling isolated from your surrounding community. Self-consciousness and fear of judgment build a wall between you and the world. Although shying away might feel like the "safer" option, it ultimately keeps you from getting to know others, and keeps others from getting to know you. Instead of feeling like part of a community, your social anxiety makes you feel like a bystander watching from the outside. This feeling of not belonging only fills you with more insecurity, and it becomes virtually impossible to join in on the fun. You lose the opportunity to connect with your neighbors. By having strategies at the ready to manage these moments, you'll be able to break through this self-designed isolation wall and more fully engage with the people around you.

Use Skill #18, SPARK (p. 64), as a blueprint for engaging with people you don't (yet) know very well.

SHARED INTERESTS. Notice something about the person that stands out and can be a conversation starter.

> *Example:*
> • **Observation:** Notice a T-shirt with a band logo, a dish they brought, or anything that catches your eye.
> • **Starter:** "That dish looks amazing! Is it a family recipe?"

PERSONAL EXPERIENCES. Relate your experiences to a shared interest, to highlight a connection between you and the other person.

> *Example: "I love cooking too! I recently tried making a similar dish. Have you always enjoyed cooking?"*

ASK OPEN-ENDED QUESTIONS. Encourage the other person to give detailed answers, keeping the conversation flowing.

> *Example: "What's one cooking tip or recipe you think everyone should know?"*

REFLECTIVE LISTENING. Mirror back their thoughts or feelings to demonstrate that you're interested in what they have to say.

> *Example: "It sounds like cooking is a real passion for you. What do you enjoy most about it?"*

KINDNESS AND HUMOR. Use compliments and lighthearted jokes to keep the mood upbeat and enjoyable. Everyone loves a little flattery and a good laugh.

> *Example: "Your cooking skills are impressive! I need to take some lessons from you so I don't burn down the neighborhood next time I bake!"*

Reflection

- How did using SPARK impact your anxiety and enjoyment of conversations?
- Did the depth and quality of interactions improve?
- How can you apply these conversation techniques to everyday settings?
- Were there positive responses to your reflective listening or humor?
- Did you feel more connected to your community after these conversations?
- Choose a couple of people you connected with and identify shared interests for future conversations.
- Any challenges or areas for improvement?

Odd One Out

It seems that lately your friends have been making plans without you. This doesn't just make you feel left out—it makes you doubt your worth as a friend and gives you the sense that you're not valued in your social circle. You start to withdraw and engage in negative self-talk, which hurts your confidence and mood. You often scroll through social media, see your friends having fun without you, and feel even more isolated. Since you assume they don't want to spend time with you, you stop reaching out to friends or inviting them to hang out. This cycle of feeling excluded and doubting yourself continues, making it hard to break free and feel confident again. It feels like everyone is moving on without you.

WHAT IS GOING ON

When you feel unvalued or disliked, it triggers a cascade of distressing emotions. Your mind races with thoughts of rejection and inadequacy, leading to a downward spiral of negative thinking. These persistent thoughts erode your self-worth, making it challenging to maintain your self-esteem. Physically, this stress can manifest as a heavy heart and a deep sense of isolation, intensifying your emotional turmoil. Recognizing these internal triggers is crucial. By actively addressing these feelings, you can rebuild your confidence and sense of belonging, ensuring that negative thoughts don't control your emotional well-being.

ADDRESS THE ISSUE

Use Skill #13 "Flip the Script" (pp. 49–50).

1. **Spot negative behaviors** that make you feel worse, like looking at your friends' social media. Commit to limiting your time on social media to prevent triggering these negative feelings.

2. **Pause and acknowledge.** Take a moment to acknowledge the feelings of exclusion and self-doubt, and note how unhelpful they are in this situation. Write down these feelings in a journal to process them constructively.

3. **Challenge your negative thoughts.** Find the opposite action. Consider what makes you feel good, such as engaging in a hobby or talking to a supportive friend. Spend time on an activity you enjoy, like painting or chatting with a friend.

4. **Commit to opposite action.** Feeling left out might make you want to isolate even more, feeling like you're a loser no one wants to spend time with. But isolating will only make you feel worse. Even if it's hard, engage in something positive and self-affirming. Call up another friend to hang out, or engage in a hobby you enjoy—especially if it's a skill you're really good at.

5. **Notice the difference.** Observe how you feel after engaging in these positive, opposite actions. Do you feel less isolated? More self-confident?

6. **Practice regularly.** Make a habit of checking in with yourself when you're doubting your worth, and integrate it into your daily interactions.

Reflection

- How did it feel to recognize and change negative behaviors?
- Did your confidence and mood improve?
- What are some activities or people that uplift you?
- What are some small steps you can take right now to counter your self-doubt?
- List a few kind, affirming statements to counter your negative self-talk.
- Keep a list of positive actions for tough times.

Keeping Track of Yourself

As your friend's game night approaches, doubts start to creep in. You start to feel anxious about meeting new people. Even though you imagine everyone will be nice, you feel uneasy. It's hard to pinpoint exactly why—all you know is that the negative thoughts are there, and they've begun to take over. You start to beat yourself up about being so socially awkward, which only makes you feel worse about yourself.

WHAT IS GOING ON

Like all bad habits, anxious thinking can take over before we even realize what's happening. It can feel so sudden and overwhelming that it's hard to even put a name on what we're feeling—let alone how to make ourselves feel better. The physical symptoms, like a knotted stomach and shaky hands, make it even more intense. You probably wouldn't be able to say if someone were to ask you, "What's wrong?" You just know something is very, very wrong.

ADDRESS THE ISSUE

The thing is, to address your social anxiety, you need to be able to get a handle on it enough to recognize when it's reared its ugly head, and why. If your thinking brain is too overwhelmed to do this, it might be time for your creative brain to step in. Use Skill #15 the "Creative Thought Tracker" (pp. 52–56) to manage these cycles of overthinking.

Reflection

- What did it feel like to engage with your anxiety creatively?
- Did giving shape and color to your thoughts make them more or less overwhelming?
- Did you notice a shift in your mood or stress level?

Wrapping It Up

You meet an old college friend at a coffee shop to catch up. You're excitedly sharing updates about your new job, recent vacation, and personal milestones. Initially, your friend listens attentively, but soon starts looking around the coffee shop and glancing at their watch. Their responses become shorter and less enthusiastic. You notice they're quiet, which makes you feel like you need to talk even more to fill the silence, and it makes you wonder if maybe you're just not very interesting. The conversation starts to feel forced, and you begin to get anxious about how to continue, which only makes you ramble more.

WHAT IS GOING ON

Social anxiety can make our conversations awkward, because we're not always able to fully connect with other people as we talk. Sometimes it's because we're lost in our own head, worried what they think about us, so we don't actively listen. Sometimes we don't know quite what to say, or don't notice subtle cues coming from other people. In this case, you missed the signals that your friend was ready to move on.

ADDRESS THE ISSUE

Use Skill #22 "When to Stop Talking" (pp. 71–72). By being more mindful of other people's reactions, you can shift an awkward conversation from nervous monologue to two-way dialogue. This awareness can ease the pressure, making interactions less stressful for you and more enjoyable for everyone.

Reflection

- Were you able to notice cues and adjust your behavior accordingly? What were some of these cues?
- Did you observe a shift in the listener's engagement or the balance of the conversation?
- What are some ways you can ensure future conversations are balanced and inclusive?
- How can you make a habit of observing verbal and nonverbal cues during conversations?
- How can you make sure the context and setting is appropriate for the interaction you're having?
- Next time you anticipate a stressful conversation, what questions can you prepare to show interest in the other person?

Checking In with Your Anxiety

You've just returned from a fishing trip with a friend. It was going great, but your friend brought along college roommates and at one point you started feeling nervous around them, unsure of what to talk to them about. You started to feel anxious trying to come up with topics, worried that you'd embarrass yourself and your friend by saying something dumb. So you stayed quiet. Then you started worrying that they'd think you were weird because you just sat there without engaging in conversation like everyone else. This thought made you even more anxious, and you found yourself falling into an anxiety spiral.

WHAT IS GOING ON

As you started overanalyzing how others perceived you, you got lost in your own thoughts and disengaged from the situation. The more anxious your thoughts, the more your body reacted—your mouth got dry, your hands got clammy, and you started to fidget uncomfortably—and it became hard to focus on what others were saying. You fell so quickly into the familiar anxiety spiral that you didn't even notice what triggered it; you just felt its overwhelming force disrupt your interactions. But self-awareness is key to managing social anxiety. Taking time to reflect after an anxiety episode can help you understand how and why it shows up in your everyday life.

ADDRESS THE ISSUE

Use Skill #23 "Daily Check-In" (pp. 73–74) to track your social anxiety over time and identify unhelpful thoughts and behavior patterns. With this self-awareness, you're better equipped to confront social anxiety head-on.

Reflection

- How did it feel to look back and rate your social interactions today?
- Did you notice any patterns or recurring themes in your anxiety levels?
- What specific goals can you set to improve your social interactions?
- How can you incorporate awareness of your anxiety, and what triggers it, into your daily routine?
- How can you continue to track your progress and adjust your strategies?

5
Dating and Romance

Dating and romance can feel like navigating a minefield when you struggle with intense insecurity. The fear of rejection, the pressure to impress, and the vulnerability of opening up can be overwhelming. What if you could apply the same tools that help manage your anxiety to these romantic scenarios? In this chapter, you will discover how techniques like mindfulness, self-reflection, and effective communication can transform your dating life. Imagine confidently approaching a date and enjoying genuine connections without constant fear holding you back. Get ready to unlock the secrets to a more fulfilling romantic journey by integrating powerful tools into your love life.

Awkward Dynamics

You have been on a few dates with someone new. Tonight, you're meeting at a charming little restaurant. As you sit across from each other, you notice your date fidgeting with their utensils and avoiding eye contact. They seem uncomfortable, which makes you worry that you're not an interesting date. You're not sure how to get them to be more engaged and at ease in the conversation. This makes you more nervous. Whenever they do engage and say something, you're distracted just trying to come up with ways to keep the conversation going. You're so wrapped up in your anxious thoughts at this point that you feel even more disconnected from them.

WHAT IS GOING ON

Your date's nervousness is evident through their body language and hesitations. This situation can be triggering as you worry about making a good impression and fear judgment or rejection. Their behavior makes you insecure, and this insecurity only makes you pull away instead of drawing the other person in. It becomes even more difficult for them to engage fully in the conversation. Instead of focusing on shifting the awkward dynamics, you become preoccupied with your faults and shortcomings. The date gets even more awkward.

ADDRESS THE ISSUE

Use Skill #2, "Active Listening" (pp. 19–21) to recognize the signs of awkward dynamics. Doing so will help you respond in a way that eases your anxiety and fosters a more relaxed and enjoyable interaction. Below is an example tailored for this particular scenario.

1. Pause your anxious thoughts and take a moment to observe the social cues the other person is sending.

- **Verbal cues.** During dinner, I noticed my date's voice was softer, and they hesitated before speaking, which seemed unusual compared to our previous conversations.

- **Nonverbal cues.** They were fidgeting with their utensils and avoiding eye contact, occasionally glancing around the restaurant, making it clear they were uneasy.

2. Demonstrate understanding.

- **Show empathy.** To show empathy, I leaned in slightly, maintained a gentle smile, and nodded to indicate that I was paying attention and understanding their nervousness. I wanted to create a safe space where they felt heard and valued.

- **Engage actively.** I asked open-ended questions like, "What have you been up to recently?" and "How was your week?" I maintained eye contact and nodded to show genuine interest in their responses, helping to keep the conversation flowing naturally.

3. Identify emotions.

- **Speaker's emotions.** My date seemed anxious and uncertain, likely feeling self-conscious or insecure about how the evening was going.

- **Underlying messages.** They might have been worried about making a good impression and were unsure how I felt about them, contributing to their nervousness.

4. Ask clarifying questions.

- As a way of reconnecting with them, I gently inquired, "You seem a bit nervous, is everything okay?" and "What's been on your mind lately?"

- **Impact on understanding.** These questions helped me understand that they were worried about how the date was going and whether I was enjoying their company. Their responses provided clarity and allowed me to address their concerns directly.

5. Summarize their main points.

- **Mirror what they've shared.** I said, "It sounds like you're interested in getting to know me better but feel nervous about making a good impression."

- **Note the speaker's response.** My date seemed relieved and appreciated my understanding and reassurance, which helped them relax and open up more during the conversation.

6. Take action.

- **Reassure.** I said, "I enjoy spending time with you, and I'm glad we're getting to know each other better."

- **Engage in shared activities.** To ease the tension further, I suggested we discuss a mutual interest, like a hobby or a recent movie we both enjoyed.

Reflection

- How did it feel to practice active listening during the date?
- Did you notice a change in your date's comfort level and engagement?
- In what other situations might these listening skills be helpful?
- How can you make a habit of applying these skills in future interactions?

Critical-Sounding Comments

Imagine that you're conversing with your partner over a homemade dinner, and they casually say, "This meal is okay, but it's not as good as the one you made last week." This comment triggers feelings of self-doubt and disappointment. Your inner critic starts filling your mind with negative thoughts about your cooking abilities and value as a partner.

WHAT IS GOING ON

When your partner casually remarks about your cooking, it activates your inner critic. This internal voice immediately starts generating negative thoughts, such as doubts about your abilities and self-worth. This situation is particularly triggering because it reinforces fears of inadequacy and failure. The inner critic's negative self-talk makes it hard to focus on the positive aspects of the interaction and can lead to heightened anxiety and self-consciousness.

ADDRESS THE ISSUE

Use Skill #3, "Getting to Know Your Inner Critic" (pp. 22–24) to managing and mitigating the impact of these negative thoughts and learn to recognize them as the inner critic's voice. Below is an example tailored for this dating/relationship scenario.

ACTION	PROMPT	YOUR NOTES
1. Identify	Think about a recent interaction where your inner critic became active. What triggered it, and what were the specific thoughts?	Example: I was triggered by my partner's comment comparing my cooking. Thoughts included, "I'm not good enough," "I can't please my partner," and "I'm failing as a partner."
2. Label	Imagine your inner critic as a separate persona. Please give it a name or label.	Example: I've named my inner critic "Critical Carl."
3. Recognize	How can you quickly recognize when your inner critic's voice arises? What trigger phrase or cue could you use?	Example: My trigger phrase is "Here comes Critical Carl."
4. Practice in real time	Visualize yourself in an anxiety-inducing setting where your inner critic speaks up. What trigger phrase or cue would you use?	Example: I can use the "Here comes Critical Carl" cue to acknowledge my inner critic. Take a deep breath and mentally note, "This is Carl speaking, not my true self."
5. Respond with compassion	How can you respond to your inner critic with self-compassion? Write a brief affirming statement.	Example: "I am doing my best, and it's okay not to be perfect. My worth is not defined by one meal."

ACTION	PROMPT	YOUR NOTES
6. Share	Consider sharing your reflections with others facing similar challenges.	Example: Share experiences with close friends or a support group, discussing strategies for overcoming negative self-talk.
7. Put awareness into action	How can you integrate this practice into daily interactions? What small actions can foster self-awareness and support among peers?	Example: I can regularly recite affirmations and encourage peers to do the same, creating a supportive environment to discuss and counteract inner critics.

Reflection

- How did it feel to recognize and label your inner critic?
- Did naming your inner critic reduce the impact of what it was telling you?
- What trigger phrases and self-compassionate affirmations can I use daily?
- Who can I share these observations with? How can I seek support in challenging my inner critic?

Biases and Making Connections

You meet someone new at a book club and instantly bond over your shared love for classic novels. However, a nagging hesitation lingers about pursuing a romantic relationship because you hold biases about their profession as an engineer. Your father was an engineer and was a very emotionally detached person, so you assume all engineers must be the same way. Despite the connection, you worry their analytical nature might overshadow the romance and spontaneity you crave. Certain that a relationship wouldn't work in the long run, you decide not to pursue a deeper connection.

WHAT IS GOING ON

Preconceived notions based on a single experience and stringent bias can keep you from getting to know the other person for who they are, and immediately closes off any possibility of a romantic relationship. Assumptions can hold you back from making a deeper connection. These patterns can make you doubt your ability to ever connect meaningfully with someone. Biases disrupt personal relationships, deepen feelings of isolation, and activate anxious thoughts.

ADDRESS THE ISSUE

Use Skill #8, the "Bias Buster" (pp. 33–36) for dismantling preconceived notions. Begin by describing a similar interaction to the above scenario.

_____

_____

_____

_____

Identify the assumptions that came up during the interaction. Record your answers in the blank spaces.

What specific bias do you have against someone?	Example: "Engineers are too logical and won't be emotionally expressive or romantic, which is important to me in a relationship."
Where did this belief originate? Is it rooted in past experiences?	Example: "My father was an engineer who emphasized rational thinking over emotional expression."
How has this belief influenced your behavior in past social interactions?	Example: "In college a guy in the engineering department asked me out, but I said no."

Challenge the evidence by assessing the facts of the situation. Record your answers in the blank spaces.

What concrete evidence do I have that supports this belief?	Example: "Only that my father was emotionally distant."
Can I remember instances where this assumption was disproven?	Example: "I've met some of my dad's coworkers at his company's family picnics, and they seem to be affectionate with their children."
Are you focusing only on details that support your bias and ignoring those contradicting it?	Example: "My dad's boss always brings his wife flowers after returning from a business trip."

Explore alternative perspectives. Open your mind to other ways of approaching this person and situation. Record your answers in the blank spaces.

What are some other ways to interpret this situation?	Example: Every person has their own personality, regardless of their profession.
How might someone with a different perspective view this same scenario?	Example: People have different "love languages," and just because someone has a different one than yours, it doesn't mean they don't have romantic feelings for you.

Consider the consequences. Ask yourself what will happen if you hold on to these biases. Record your answers in the blank spaces.

How do these beliefs affect your emotions and behaviors?	
How will holding on to these assumptions in the long term affect your relationships and mental health?	
What might change for the better if I altered my perspective?	

Challenge logical fallacies. Examine your thought patterns. Record your answers in the blank spaces.

Am I engaging in black-and-white thinking?	Example: "Yes, I am seeing all engineers as unromantic."
Am I overgeneralizing from a few experiences?	Example: "Yes, I'm assuming all engineers are like my father."
Am I catastrophizing potential outcomes unnecessarily?	Example: "Yes, I'm jumping to the conclusion that I'll never have a long-term relationship."

Seek resolution. Once you've gone through and fact-checked your biases, ask yourself the following questions and record your answers in the blank spaces.

What new insights have I gained about my social fears?	Example: "I've learned that my fears are based on stereotypes, not facts. Moving forward, I'll focus on our shared interests and the positive aspects of their personality rather than their job title."
How can I use this new understanding to approach social situations more confidently?	Example: "I can fact-check my assumptions when I notice them taking hold."
What steps can I take to challenge and change my biases in future interactions?	Example: "I can continue to challenge my biases in my future interactions with engineers."

Reflection

- How did it feel to identify and challenge your biases?
- Did exploring alternative perspectives change how you view the situation?
- How can you avoid letting biases affect your future interactions?
- How can you encourage others to address and challenge their biases constructively?

Repeating the Past

You've been on a few dates that didn't go well. One date ended awkwardly when you ran out of things to discuss, and another ended abruptly when your date seemed uninterested. Reflecting on these experiences, you start thinking, "I always ruin relationships." This thought triggers feelings of inadequacy and fear of future failures, making you hesitant to pursue new relationships. You worry that your past failures will repeat themselves, and you avoid social situations where you might meet potential partners.

WHAT IS GOING ON

Negative self-talk can stem from past dating experiences that didn't go as planned. This thought pattern can trigger your social anxiety, leading you to believe you are incapable of maintaining relationships. Such thoughts can become self-fulfilling prophecies—they make you more anxious and you're then likely to behave in ways that hinder relationship success. Understanding and addressing these thoughts is crucial for breaking the cycle of negativity and opening up to new possibilities.

ADDRESS THE ISSUE

Use Skill #14, CLEAR (p. 51) to stop negative thoughts in its tracks.

CHALLENGE. Notice and challenge the pervasive thought, "I always ruin relationships."

Example: "Realizing 'I always ruin relationships' is an exaggeration. There were times when things went well."

LEARN. Pay attention to when and why these thoughts arise and how they make you feel.

Example: "These thoughts usually surface after a disappointing date or a lonely moment, triggered by past failures."

EVALUATE. Assess the evidence supporting these negative thoughts.

Example: "Reflecting on the past, I see that not all my dating experiences have ended poorly. Some were quite successful."

ADJUST. Modify your thinking if the self-critical thought isn't wholly accurate.

Example: "I'll remind myself of the positive dating experiences to counterbalance the few negative ones."

REFRAME. Change your internal narrative from "I always mess up" to "Sometimes things don't go as planned, but I've also had successes."

Example: "I will start acknowledging that while some interactions were less than perfect, many have been positive."

Reflection

- How else has negative self-talk affected your romantic relationships?
- Was it easy to challenge these thoughts?
- How can you make a habit of recognizing and reframing negative self-talk?

Navigating Social Cues

Imagine you're at a speed-dating event, heart pounding with a mix of excitement and nervousness. You step into the room and see people mingling, laughing, and chatting in small groups. You want to make a good impression but are unsure how to dive into conversations and connect with others. You get overwhelmed and end up just standing to the side by yourself.

WHAT IS GOING ON

The pressure to make quick connections can be daunting in a setting like this. For someone dealing with social anxiety, the fear of rejection and the need to perform well in a short amount of time can heighten feelings of self-doubt and nervousness. Understanding and navigating social cues is crucial to feeling more at ease and making the most of the event.

ADDRESS THE ISSUE

We will use Skill #20 "Catch the VIBE" (pp. 67–68) to navigate this or another similar stressful scenario.

VISUAL SCAN. Start by visually scanning the room. Notice the layout and where people are gathering.

- Example: Look for clusters of people near the snack table, small groups seated, or mingling near the entrance. Spotting the friendliest-looking group makes you feel a bit more comfortable.

- Tip: Make it a game! See how quickly you can spot the friendliest-looking group or the most animated conversation.

INDICATORS OF MOOD. Pay attention to the general mood and energy of the room. Listen for laughter, animated chatter, or quieter conversations.

- Example: Are people laughing and chatting excitedly, or are they more subdued and quietly engaged? You notice that the room feels energetic, with lots of laughter and animated conversations, which helps you match your mood to the room's vibe.

- Tip: Try to match your mood to the room's vibe. If it's lively, let yourself feel more energetic; if it's calm, embrace the tranquility.

BODY LANGUAGE. Observe body language to gauge openness and engagement.

- Example: Are people leaning in toward each other and making eye contact, or are they turned away and avoiding interaction? Seeing people leaning in, making eye contact, and smiling, you mimic these positive body language cues to feel more connected.

- Tip: Mimic the positive body language you see. If someone looks relaxed and open, adopt a similar posture.

ENGAGEMENT LEVELS. Assess how involved people are in their conversations. High engagement suggests interest, while low engagement might indicate boredom.

- Example: Are people deeply engrossed in conversation or looking around the room and checking their phones? You notice that most people seem deeply engaged in their discussions, so you approach someone who looks friendly and ask a simple question like, "How are you finding the event so far?" This breaks the ice and starts a pleasant conversation.

- Tip: Engage in a brief, low-stakes interaction. Ask someone a simple question about the event or comment on the surroundings.

Reflection

- Did you notice a shift in your mood as you observed without making judgement or assumptions?
- How did it feel to use the VIBE method to navigate the room?
- Did identifying the room's mood and body language help reduce your anxiety?
- What steps can you take to practice the VIBE method in other social settings?
- What can you do to approach future interactions with an open and positive attitude?

Breaking into the Convo

Imagine you're on a first date at a cozy bar. The ambiance is perfect, with soft lighting and a gentle hum of background chatter. Your date is enthusiastic and dives into discussing their interests and experiences, ranging from their latest travel adventures to their passion for cooking. You find it hard to get a word in as they speak. You start to feel overwhelmed by the intensity of the conversation. You want to contribute and share your thoughts but struggle to find the right moment. You're worried about interrupting them or coming across as rude, but you also need a break to collect your thoughts and regain your composure.

WHAT IS GOING ON

In this scenario, the one-sided nature of the conversation can be particularly overwhelming. When your date dominates the conversation, it can trigger feelings of anxiety and inadequacy. This is common for anyone who feels pressured to engage meaningfully but is unsure how do it. The fear of offending your date or disrupting the flow of conversation adds to the anxiety. Finding a strategy to manage the situation gracefully and create space for yourself is essential to ensuring the date remains enjoyable for both parties.

ADDRESS THE ISSUE

Use Skill #24, PAUSE (p. 75) to navigate this conversation.

POLITELY INTERRUPT. Gently insert a pause into the conversation.

> *Example: Wait for a slight pause in your date's story and say, "Sorry to interrupt, but I just remembered something I wanted to ask you."*

ACKNOWLEDGE THE INTERACTION. Show appreciation for the conversation.

Example: "I've enjoyed our chat," or "It's cool that we have a lot in common."

USE AN EXCUSE. Provide a reason for needing to take a break or change the subject.

Example: "Excuse me, I just have to make a quick call."

SUGGEST FUTURE CONTACT. Offer to reconnect later or continue the conversation later.

Example: "I've gotta head out, but let's catch up again soon."

EXIT GRACEFULLY. End with a polite gesture and farewell.

Example: "I had a great time, take care!"

Reflection

- How did using the PAUSE method to manage the conversation feel?
- Did politely interrupting and acknowledging the conversation help ease your anxiety?
- In what other social settings or low-stakes conversations can I practice the PAUSE method?
- What worked well? What step do I need to work on?

6
Work and School

We spend most of our day at work or school, yet these settings can feel like minefields of potentially anxiety-inducing scenarios. This chapter explores how to handle everyday challenges, from interactions with colleagues and classmates to building emotional resilience. Learn how to cultivate a sense of calm, assertiveness, and self-assurance in professional and academic settings. By integrating these techniques, you can move through your work and school life more efficiently, turning anxiety into a stepping-stone for success.

Building Your Network

You're attending a networking event for professionals in your industry. As you enter the venue, you notice groups of people deeply engaged in conversations, exchanging business cards, and laughing easily. The room hums with confidence and camaraderie. You clutch your business cards, but an overwhelming dread creeps in. Your mind races: "I don't have as much experience or expertise as these other professionals. They probably won't take me seriously." The thought of approaching a group and introducing yourself feels terrifying. You stand at the edge of the room, feeling increasingly isolated as you watch others network effortlessly. You start to fear that your career will never advance.

WHAT IS GOING ON

Networking events can be a significant trigger for social anxiety. The roomful of confident professionals amplifies feelings of inadequacy. The mind becomes a battleground of negative thoughts, such as "I'm not experienced enough" and "They won't take me seriously." These thoughts stem from a fear of judgment and rejection. The body reacts with physical symptoms like a racing heart, sweaty palms, and a tight stomach, further escalating the feelings of anxiety. Seeing others effortlessly engaging in conversations can make you feel like an outsider, heightening fears of being dismissed or judged harshly. This paralyzing anxiety creates a barrier, making it challenging to initiate conversations or participate in the event.

ADDRESS THE ISSUE

We will use Skill #10, "Reframing Anxious Thoughts" (pp. 40–42).

1. **Begin by identifying the negative thoughts.**

   Example: "I don't have as much experience. They won't take me seriously."

2. **Question the evidence.** Ask yourself, "What proof do I have that these thoughts are true? Is there another way to view this situation?

   Example: "I have valuable experience. Everyone starts somewhere."

3. **Consider alternative perspectives.** Might other people be more focused on their concerns than on judging you?

   Example: "Others might be nervous too. They're likely concentrating on their own goals."

4. **Challenge catastrophic thinking.** What's the worst that could realistically happen? How probable is it?

   Example: "The worst is someone not showing interest, which isn't personal. It's unlikely everyone will dismiss me."

5. **Generate counterarguments.** What contradicts your negative thoughts? Have you handled similar situations successfully before?

   Example: "I've had successful conversations at past events. My skills are valuable."

6. **Reframe negative thoughts.** How can you rephrase this negative thought?

   Example: "I have valuable insights and am here to learn and connect."

7. **Practice positive self-talk.** What positive statements can I use?

   Example: "I am capable." "My company had enough confidence to send me here to represent them."

8. **Visualize success.** What would a positive interaction look like?

   Example: Picture engaging in meaningful conversations and confidently exchanging business cards.

9. **Practice mindfulness.** What techniques can I use to calm my anxious thoughts?

   Example: Focus on your breath, observe without judgment, and listen actively.

10. **Celebrate progress.** Acknowledge the moments when you were able to connect with other attendees.

    Example: "I had a good conversation over lunch about challenges in our industry."

Reflection

- How did it feel to challenge and reframe your negative thoughts?
- How can you incorporate these techniques in other professional settings?
- Are there any smaller, less intimidating settings where you can practice and build more confidence?

Participation Jitters

You're a college student embarking on a new semester. You're excited, but also apprehensive. Large lecture halls and group projects loom on the horizon. The thought of speaking up in class or collaborating with peers sends your heart racing. You begin to doubt that you're a good student at all, and worry that you might not get good enough grades to keep your scholarship.

WHAT IS GOING ON

Settings where participation and interaction are required can be particularly anxiety-inducing. Many students feel pressured to perform well academically while navigating complicated social dynamics. The fear of being judged or making mistakes can result in negative self-talk and avoidance. By addressing the root causes of your anxiety and employing compassionate self-talk, you can learn to manage the stress more effectively so you can be fully present for your college experience.

ADDRESS THE ISSUE

We will use Skill #4, "Mastering a Compassionate Mindset" (pp. 25–26).

1. **Identify triggers.** Write down triggers like "Feeling anxious about participating in large classes" and "Fear of judgment in group projects."

_____

_____

_____

2. **Acknowledge feelings.** "I am feeling anxious about tomorrow's lecture," or "I am being too hard on myself about the group project."

3. **Challenge negative thoughts.** Replace "I'm going to mess up and everyone will judge me" with "Mistakes are part of learning and growing."

4. **Speak kindly to yourself.** Use phrases like "I am proud of myself for stepping out of my comfort zone" and "Imperfection is part of being human, and I embrace my journey."

5. **Use affirmations.** Remind yourself "I deserve compassion from myself and others," and "I am capable, even in moments of anxiety."

6. **Reflect on your practice.** "After using compassionate self-talk, I felt more at ease during the lecture" and "Challenging my negative thoughts helped me contribute more to my group project."

7. **Share.** Sharing your challenges and victories can inspire others and deepen your understanding.

Reflection

- How did it feel to challenge and reframe your negative thoughts?
- How can you integrate these techniques into your routine?
- What compassionate affirmations can you have at the ready for the next time these anxious feelings arise?

Pressure to Perform Well

You've finally landed an interview for your dream job at a prestigious company. As you enter the towering office building, excitement and nervousness overwhelm you. This opportunity could change every-thing. You want to make the best impression possible. The stakes are high, and your mind races with thoughts of potential success and fear of failure.

WHAT IS GOING ON

The pressure to perform well can make maintaining a calm and com-posed demeanor challenging. Physiologically, stress can manifest as shakiness and shallow breathing, undermining confidence. Psy-chologically, the fear of failure and the desire to impress can lead to negative self-talk and doubts about your abilities. You can feel your body almost shrinking with fear, as if you're cowering in a corner hid-ing from a dragon. Adopting a power pose before an interview can help mitigate these symptoms. Power poses are body postures that take up space and open the body, signaling confidence and reduc-ing stress. By consciously adopting a confident posture, you can trick your brain into feeling more assured and less anxious.

ADDRESS THE ISSUE

In this high-stakes scenario, use Skill #19, "Power Posing" (pp. 65–66). Imagine you are standing outside the interview room, butterflies fluttering madly in your stomach. You decide to take a moment to ground yourself before stepping in. You can do these in a stairwell away from view, or in a private bathroom.

Stand tall: You find a quiet corner and stand with your feet shoulder-width apart. You straighten your spine and imagine a string pulling you upward, lifting your chest.

Open posture: You uncross your arms and legs, letting your body open up. Your hands rest comfortably by your sides, and you feel more expansive.

Wide stance: You widen your stance slightly, planting your feet firmly on the ground. You feel more stable and grounded.

Expansive gestures: You practice using your hands to gesture as you speak, avoiding crossing your arms. This makes you feel more dynamic and expressive. Recite something that you hope to share with your interviewer in this way.

Head held high: You keep your head up, with your chin parallel to the ground, projecting confidence.

Eye contact: As you visualize the interview, you practice making friendly, confident eye contact with the interviewer.

Smile: You wear a genuine smile, which helps you feel more positive and relaxed.

Breathe deeply: You take slow, deep breaths, inhaling through your nose and exhaling through your mouth, releasing any lingering tension.

Visualize your power: You take a moment to visualize yourself succeeding in the interview, answering questions confidently and engaging positively with the interviewers.

Practice regularly: Make a habit of noticing when your anxiety is showing up physically, and keep track of your progress.

DATE	OBSERVATION	PROGRESS
04/01/2024	Practiced power poses before the interview. Felt more grounded and confident. Made good eye contact and used expansive gestures.	Felt less anxious and more composed.
04/02/2024	Reflected on yesterday's interview. Noticed improved posture and confidence during the conversation.	Continued practice for the following interview.
04/03/2024	Practiced deep breathing and visualization. Felt positive and prepared for the follow-up interview.	Reduced anxiety and increased self-assurance.

Reflection

- Did adjusting your posture help you feel more comfortable?
- Did you notice any difference in how you were perceived by the interviewer? Did you receive positive feedback or notice more engagement?
- What are some other high-stress, high-stakes situations where power posing might be helpful?
- What can I do to cultivate awareness of how my anxiety shows up in my body and posture?

Anxious Afterthoughts

After attending a networking event, you find yourself caught in a whirlwind of thoughts. Pride mingles with doubt as you replay the conversations in your mind. You felt a surge of confidence when you initiated discussions with new contacts, but now you're questioning if you appeared self-assured enough. Did you leave a good impression? Were your interactions as smooth as they seemed? These nagging doubts linger, making it hard to move on and focus on the positives.

WHAT IS GOING ON

Post-event rumination is a familiar struggle for those with social anxiety. The event is over, but your mind is on replay, dissecting each moment. This mental loop can magnify perceived flaws and overshadow your successes. The anxiety of potentially being harshly judged fuels these thoughts, creating a barrier to constructive reflection. Even though the physical symptoms of stress—like a pounding headache or an irritated stomach—have faded, the emotional residue persists, making it challenging to celebrate achievements or learn from the experience.

ADDRESS THE ISSUE

Use Skill #12, "Event Reflection Ritual" (pp. 46–48) after a networking event to prepare your sanctuary space and focus on the positives. Below is an example specific to this scenario.

1. Settle into the moment.

   - **Choose a time.** Find a spot: Select a peaceful corner in your home, free from distractions.

   - **Set the mood.** Light a soothing candle and play gentle music to create a tranquil atmosphere.

2. Start with mindfulness.

   - **Breathe deeply.** Take several deep breaths to center yourself.

   - **Relax.** Close your eyes, release immediate stress, and focus solely on breathing.

3. Recall the event.

   - **Visualize.** Picture the venue, the people you met, and the conversations you had.

   - **Write.** Let your thoughts and emotions flow onto the page.

   - **Include specific event details.** "The event was at an elegant hotel. I networked with three new contacts about industry trends and exchanged business cards."

4. Highlight the positives.

   - **Reflect.** Note any moments of joy, connection, or accomplishment.

   - **Note the positive moments.** "I had an engaging discussion with a potential mentor. I introduced myself confidently to a group of professionals."

   - **Celebrate.** Acknowledge and savor these positive experiences.

5. Face the challenges.

   - **Identify.** Write about any awkward or anxiety-inducing moments.

   - **Grow.** View these challenges as opportunities for personal growth.

   - **Challenges faced.** "I felt uneasy joining a conversation. I stumbled over my words when discussing my experience."

6. Gain insights.

- **Ask.** What did I learn about myself? What strengths did I demonstrate? What can I improve for future interactions?

- **Write.** Capture these insights and lessons. "I learned I can initiate conversations despite nervousness. I need to practice articulating my experience more clearly."

7. Set goals.

- **Define.** Write down specific actions or skills to develop for future networking.

- **Plan.** Create a step-by-step plan to achieve these goals. "Refine my introduction. Attend more networking events to build confidence."

8. Challenge negative thoughts.

- **Notice.** Be mindful of repetitive or negative thoughts.

- **Redirect.** Practice self-compassion and refocus on the present.

- **Write.** Jot down some of these negative thoughts to diminish their power.

- **Reframe negative thoughts.** Shift the thought "I wasn't confident enough" to "'Initiating conversations shows confidence and courage.'"

9. Express gratitude.

- **Reflect.** Consider some of the positives from the event.

- **Write.** "I'm grateful for the chance to meet new people and the encouraging feedback I received."

Reflection

- How did it feel to complete this reflection ritual?
- Were you able to quiet some of the rumination and shift your mood?
- How can you make this reflection a regular anti-anxiety routine?

Stress on the Job

You're at work, and the clock is ticking. Deadlines are looming, meetings are back-to-back, and your email inbox is overflowing. The pressure is mounting, and you can feel the stress inside you. Your mind is racing, and it's hard to focus. You need to regain your composure and clarity, but don't know how. You consider saying that you're feeling sick so you can just go home for the day. Your mind starts to race with thoughts that you'll get fired because you're not good at your job.

WHAT IS GOING ON

In a busy office environment, constant demands, tight deadlines, and frequent interruptions can easily lead to overwhelm. The anxious mind interprets stress as an existential threat, triggering the body's fight or flight response.

ADDRESS THE ISSUE

Use a simple breathing exercise like Skill #6, "Ocean Breath Technique" (pp. 29–30) to activate the body's relaxation response. This helps slow the heart rate, deepen breathing, and relax the muscles. Breathing exercises can also shift your focus away from stressful thoughts, giving your mind a break and helping you regain mental clarity.

Reflection

- Did your stress levels shift? How did your focus and calmness improve?
- Did you have any difficulty focusing on your breath?
- How can you integrate this breathing practice into your daily routine during stressful times?

Fear of Future Criticism

You're a graduate student in biology, preparing to present your research at a prestigious conference. You've spent months meticulously gathering data and crafting your presentation. As the event approaches, your anxiety grows. You worry about stumbling over your words, forgetting key points, or being harshly judged by your peers and professors. The night before the conference, you lie awake, your mind racing with the fear that you're not made for this career.

WHAT IS GOING ON

Recalling past embarrassments or anticipating harsh judgments creates a cycle of negative thoughts and can be physically triggering.

ADDRESS THE ISSUE

Use Skill #5 "A Path to Self-Forgiveness" (pp. 27–28) to apply some self-compassion. Doing so helps break this cycle by calming your nervous system and fostering a sense of inner peace. It also brings you back to the present moment, and out of your anxiety-fueled head. This shift allows you to approach your presentation with confidence and clarity.

Reflection

- How did it feel to practice self-forgiveness?
- Did your feelings or physical symptoms, like muscle tension or dry mouth, change?
- How can you incorporate a regular self-forgiveness practice into your day?

7
Community

Engaging in community activities can be both exciting and daunting. From local events to casual encounters with neighbors, these interactions can bring feelings of anxiety and self-doubt, often leading to isolation. This chapter is dedicated to helping you navigate community interactions with confidence. We'll provide practical tools and strategies to manage anxiety, engage positively, and turn discomfort into personal growth. Mastering these techniques will enhance your sense of belonging and build deeper connections within your community. Discover how to thrive in your social landscape.

Speaking Up

You're a dedicated member of a community organization that plans events and activities for residents. Your involvement in this group is motivated by a desire to foster community spirit and collaboration. However, recently, you've noticed a troubling pattern during the planning meetings. One of your fellow members consistently dominates the discussions, steering decisions without seeking or considering input from others. This behavior has led to an atmosphere where some members feel marginalized and their voices unheard. You've seen firsthand how newer or quieter members hesitate to share their ideas or opinions. The situation is starting to create tension within the group, and the quality of your collective decisions is suffering. You want to address the issue, but you're afraid it will only end in conflict and bad energy, and other members will see you as an annoyance.

WHAT IS GOING ON

In this scenario, the dominant behavior of one member is disrupting the group's balance. The fear of being ignored or dismissed exacerbates the fear of speaking up, and this makes it hard for you to actively participate in the dialogue. This dynamic hinders individual contributions and affects the group's effectiveness and cohesion.

ADDRESS THE ISSUE

Use Skill #17, "Blueprint for Assertive Communication" (pp. 60–63). To address this type of issue, assertive communication is essential. It ensures all members feel valued and heard, promoting a more inclusive and collaborative atmosphere.

Reflection

- How did it feel to use assertive communication in this situation?
- Did group dynamics change after expressing your needs?
- What other situations in your life could improve through this kind of communication?

Family Drama

You're at a family gathering where tension is high. Despite your best efforts to stay calm and navigate the difficult conversations, you feel emotionally drained and overwhelmed by the night's end. Every word feels like a potential trigger, and maintaining your composure seems like a Herculean task. It feels like family members are talking over each other, with everyone just trying to win an argument.

WHAT IS GOING ON

Family gatherings can be a minefield of unresolved issues and heightened emotions. When tensions are high, conversations can quickly spiral out of control, stressing and overwhelming participants. These interactions can be particularly exhausting for someone who values harmony and strives to maintain peace. The emotional turmoil from these events can linger, making it crucial to find a way to regain inner peace and prepare for future interactions. Active listening can play a pivotal role in navigating these conversations, helping to better understand others and fostering a sense of connection and resolution.

ADDRESS THE ISSUE

Use Skill #2, "Active Listening" (pp. 19–21). To begin, take some time to describe a difficult family conversation that came up recently.

Example: There was a heated discussion over dinner about holiday plans. You wanted to go on a group trip, but your brother and his wife wanted to host the whole family at their house.

_____

_____

_____

_____

Verbal cues
Example: People raised their voices, and the arguments became repetitive

Nonverbal cues
Example: My brother crossed his arms, furrowed his brows, and avoided eye contact whenever I tried to make a point.

Show empathy
Example: Acknowledge that he's feeling burnt out from work and doesn't feel like traveling: "I understand how you feel about taking a trip away from home."

Engage
Example: Ask open-ended questions like, "Can you tell me more about your concerns?"

Speaker's emotions
Example: Detected frustration, sadness, and anger from family members about feeling unheard.

Underlying messages
Example: I sensed that he felt that since I only work part-time, I might not understand his level of burnout. It also seemed like he was feeling a little pressured by his wife.

Ask clarifying questions
Example: "Are you concerned that we might overschedule ourselves?" "Is it that you don't want to deal with the airport?"

New understanding Example: I understood better that he just didn't want to deal with any of the planning and logistics, and that he felt excluded from the decision to travel.	
Main points Example: "Sounds like you're upset because you felt ignored when we were making plans, right?" "I understand you don't want to feel overwhelmed on vacation."	
Response Example: The speaker felt heard and appreciated the effort to understand, leading to a calmer conversation.	

Reflection

- How Did Using Active Listening Change the Dynamic of the Conversation?
- What Was the Most Challenging Part of Listening Actively?
- Was It Hard to Show Empathy During Conflict?
- How Can You Incorporate Active Listening into Your Daily Interactions to Improve Communication?

Find the Enjoyment

You've been feeling stressed with work deadlines and personal responsibilities. You tend to wake up, go to work, come home, watch TV or read, go to bed, and do it all again. This routine leaves you feeling like you're not enjoying much of life, and focusing only on work leaves you feeling personally unsatisfied. On top of that, you're somewhat new to the area and haven't taken the time to get to know new people. But you get anxious with just the thought of going to a local bar or event to try to socialize with strangers. You're left feeling stressed out, unfulfilled, and isolated.

WHAT IS GOING ON

Your current routine is not conducive to relaxation or social connection. But it doesn't have to be like this! There are ways to reconnect with yourself and others in moments of stress; you just have to identify them and put them into practice. Think about non-work activities you enjoy. Let's take gardening—it's been a therapeutic escape for you in the past. You feel a sense of peace when you spend time in nature away from computer and TV screens, and nurturing seedlings into thriving plants gives you a sense of accomplishment. You love gardening so much, it's one of the few topics you feel comfortable talking about with random people. Whether it's getting advice on the best time to lay seeds, or giving others recommendations for eco-friendly fertilizers, you've always felt camaraderie with fellow gardening nerds. You look into it and it turns out there's a local gardening club that meets regularly. Now consider how you can incorporate this joyful and fulfilling activity in your life.

Use Skill #7, "Finding Calm Through Hobbies" (pp. 31–32). We'll use the gardening example to create a positive routine.

1. **Start with a morning reflection (5 minutes).** Take time before work to enjoy your garden. You can take breakfast there, or do a quick grounding meditation to feel grounded. The idea is to begin the day by feeling connected to something that calms you, creating an anxiety buffer as you start the day.

2. **Midday hobby break (15–30 minutes).** If you work from home, take lunch in your garden. Observe how the plants have grown, pull some weeds, enjoy the space you've created. If you work in an office, take a walk and observe other gardens in the area to get ideas for your own.

3. **Evening wind-down (20 minutes).** Use this hobby to help you unwind and process the day's events. Set time aside to actively engage with your garden as a way to decompress from another stressful day at work. Reflect on how you feel afterward.

4. **Weekly exploration (1 hour per week).** Dedicate an hour each week to exploring a new aspect of your hobby. Plant a new type of flower or vegetable. Attend a meeting of your local gardening club. Allow this to be a time of curiosity and growth.

5. **Mindful engagement.** Practice mindfulness while gardening. Focus on the soil's texture, plant colors, and nature's sounds, anchoring yourself in the present moment.

6. **Gratitude log (5 minutes before bed).** Write three things you're grateful for from your hobby sessions. Perhaps it's the peace from gardening, a new bloom, or connections with fellow gardeners.

Reflection

- Keep a journal to track your progress and see the positive effects over time.
- How has this hobby affected your stress and anxiety levels?
- Have you felt more connected to your community?
- What small, achievable gardening goals can you set, like planting new flowers or learning new techniques?

No One's Laughing at You

You're attending a neighborhood barbecue for the first time. The sun is shining, the smell of grilled food fills the air, and laughter rings out from various corners of the park. As you enter the event, you clutch the dish you brought, feeling excited and nervous. You notice a group of people talking and laughing together and immediately, a wave of self-consciousness washes over you. You start thinking, "They must be talking about me, judging my appearance, and wondering why I even came."

WHAT IS GOING ON

Entering a social event where you don't know many people can be daunting. Seeing others laughing and chatting can easily trigger deep insecurities. This experience is often a result of "mind reading," where you project your fears and assumptions onto others' actions without concrete evidence. This anxious thought pattern can then cause you to feel isolated and unwelcome. It's crucial to recognize and challenge these automatic thoughts so you can feel more confident in social settings.

ADDRESS THE ISSUE

Use Skill #11, "Reality Check" (pp. 43–45).

1. **Notice when you're mind reading.** Be aware of what triggers the insecurity, and what negative thoughts and feelings arise.

   - As you enter the barbecue, you see that other people are actively engaged. You worry that you're not going to have anything interesting to say.

   - Your heart races, and you feel too nervous to strike up conversations.

- When people laugh, you assume they're laughing at how awkward you are. You notice you feel anxious because you feel like you don't belong.

2. **Question your assumptions.**

   - Pause and ask yourself, "Do I have proof that they are talking about me?"

   - "Have I really done or said anything to make people dislike me?"

3. **Consider alternative explanations.**

   - Perhaps they're sharing a funny story or discussing something unrelated to you. Remind yourself that people laugh for many reasons.

   - Maybe they're not ignoring you—they're just so caught up in their conversations they didn't notice you come in.

4. **Focus on facts.**

   - Ground yourself in reality by acknowledging, "The only fact I know is that people are laughing. I don't know why, and that's okay."

   - Take note of their actions toward you. Other than laugh among themselves, have they done anything to directly express their dislike toward you?

   - I've had pleasant interactions with that neighbor. There's no reason why they'd start being mean now.

5. **Challenge negative thoughts.**

   - Instead of thinking, "They must be laughing at me," tell yourself, "I don't know what they're thinking, but I'm here to enjoy myself and meet new people."

- "Hey, looks like they're having fun. I should join that conversation."

- "I've been wrong before about people laughing at me. Maybe I'm wrong now."

6. **Practice self-compassion.**

   - Remind yourself, "It's normal to feel nervous at a new event. I'll be kind to myself and take things one step at a time."

   - If necessary, find a sanctuary space to gather yourself and breathe through the anxiety and negative self-talk.

Reflection

- Did challenging your assumptions make it easier to engage at the barbecue?
- Did focusing on facts improve your interactions and enjoyment?
- How can you use these steps to manage anxiety in future situations?

Anxiety over Daily Tasks

You're buying your weekly groceries and pushing the shopping cart down the crowded aisles of the grocery store. The bright fluorescent lights, packed shelves, and background noise of other shoppers create a chaotic environment. As you walk through the store, thoughts bombard your mind: "I should buy only healthy foods," "I mustn't spend too much money," "I should hurry up."

WHAT IS GOING ON

In situations like this, the internal pressure to make perfect choices, combined with an over-stimulating environment, can stop you in your tracks with anxiety, making the simple tasks like grocery shopping feel overwhelming and stressful. Thoughts like "I should only buy healthy foods" create unrealistic expectations, setting the set the stage for guilt or regret. By recognizing and transforming these thoughts, you can loosen the grip of your inner critic and learn to manage daily tasks with greater ease and self-compassion.

ADDRESS THE ISSUE

Use Skill #16, "Flex Your Mind" (pp. 57–58). First, take note of the "should" thoughts as they arise, and how they make you feel.

1. **Ask yourself: Is this realistic?** "Is it realistic to only buy healthy foods all the time? Is it fair to demand perfection from myself?" "Am I only setting myself up for disappointment when I give in to that chocolate craving?"

2. **Change the thought.** Change "I must only buy healthy foods" to "It's okay to buy a mix of healthy foods and treats."

3. **Be kind to yourself.** Remind yourself, "It's normal to have cravings, and it's okay to enjoy treats occasionally."

4. **Set achievable goals.** Decide to buy primarily healthy foods, but allow yourself a few treats. Celebrate the balance you achieved in your choices.

5. **Practice, practice, practice!** Each time you shop, practice these steps. Over time, you'll find it easier to navigate your thoughts with compassion and flexibility.

Reflection

- How did changing your "should" thoughts impact your experience?
- Where else in your life do these "should" thoughts show up?
- How can you apply these steps to other areas of your life?

Leaving a Good Impression

You're attending an event for local business owners, hoping to meet new clients and potential partners. You spot several individuals you'd like to approach, but a wave of anxiety hits you. Since you're representing your business, it's important to project self-confidence and friendliness, but you're not sure how to do that. Your hands feel clammy, and you become hyper-aware of your posture and movements. Doubts creep into your mind.

WHAT IS GOING ON

Social interactions are particularly stressful if there's an added pressure of creating meaningful or "productive" connections that leave a good impression. A crowded, bustling environment can heighten feelings of self-consciousness, and physical symptoms of anxiety can show up in your body language. If your hands feel clammy, you may avoid shaking hands. If you're feeling self-conscious, you may look around the room while talking, making it seem like you're uninterested in the other person. These anxiety behaviors can send the wrong social cues and turn people off, or simply keep you from engaging fully with them. Eye contact is a key component of body language. Mastering it under stressful circumstances will help you interact more effectively with potential contacts.

ADDRESS THE ISSUE

Use Skill #21, "Eye See You" (pp. 69–70) to improve our body language during conversations.

Mirror magic: Stand in front of a mirror and give yourself a pep talk while maintaining eye contact with your reflection.

Example: Before the event, look yourself in the eyes and affirm your reason for going. "My business is a great contribution to the community." "I can make meaningful connections today with other business owners." "I have interesting ideas for expanding my business." Let these affirmations build your confidence by maintaining eye contact as you repeat them.

Friendship face-off: The day before the event, ask a friend or family member to help you face your nerves.

Example: Sit facing each other and take turns making silly faces at each other while maintaining eye contact. Have a couple things in mind that you want to tell people at this event, like "I hope to partner with other businesses so we can create more local jobs" or "I've been thinking about organizing a job fair for young people." As your friend distracts you, practice calmly sharing these points while maintaining eye contact. Like this, you'll have a sense of how to overcome your nervousness in a way that lets you communicate and connect in a self-assured way.

Triangle trick: Recruit a friend or family member to pose as a potential competitor. You want to find out more about their business, but feel nervous about asking questions.

Example: As you're talking with them and asking about their business, focus on the triangle between their eyes and nose to focus your gaze. Ask for feedback from your friend—did your eye contact feel awkward, or natural? Did you come off as threatening, or friendly? Once you've figured out what works, use this technique to maintain eye contact without feeling overwhelmed.

Balance connection quest: You're in a culturally diverse area, so you want to make sure you properly communicate with different community members. Research differences in communication styles between your culture and those different than yours.

Example: Get a sense of who may be attending the event beforehand. If there will be people from different backgrounds, read up on norms around eye contact and body language in their cultures. This isn't just to make sure you behave "correctly"—it's also to make sure you don't misinterpret other people's body language as a sign of disinterest or hostility. It's possible, for example, that someone else sees sustained eye contact as threatening, and avoid it as a sign of respect or kindness.

Reflection rave: After the event, celebrate your progress and release the stress.

Example: Put on your favorite song, dance around, and give yourself a high-five in the mirror while maintaining eye contact. Let yourself relax—you did a good job!

Reflection

- Was it challenging to maintain eye contact when nervous or distracted?
- Did your interactions improve with better eye contact?
- How can you integrate these exercises into your daily interactions?

Conclusion

As you close this book, acknowledge the progress you've already made in mastering social anxiety. With practice, the skills and insight you gain will help you transform your life. Embrace the strides you've taken to silence your inner critic. When self-doubt whispers, counter it with affirmations and uplifting self-talk. Treat yourself with the compassion and kindness you deserve.

Every conversation, no matter how brief, is a triumph. These interactions build your confidence and ease your anxiety. Move at your own pace, and celebrate each victory, no matter how small. Each one marks a significant step forward.

Overthinking might still challenge you, but mindfulness is your secret weapon. Regular mindfulness practice anchors you in the present, helping you break free from the cycle of overthinking. When your mind starts to spiral into regret about the past or anxiety about the future, gently guide it back to the here and now.

Believe in your extraordinary ability to grow and adapt. Be patient with yourself, knowing that setbacks are just milestones to more significant progress. Whenever you need a reminder or a boost, revisit these pages. Practice regular self-reflection—it will help you identify what works and doesn't work for you.

Your future is bright and filled with endless possibilities. Believe in yourself and embrace the path ahead with confidence and optimism.

References

American Psychological Association. *Journal of Personality and Social Psychology.* (May 2024). Retrieved from https://www.apa.org/pubs/journals/psp

Brooks, Alison Wood, Julianna Schroeder, Jane Risen, Francesca Gino, Adam D. Galinsky, Michael I. Norton, and Maurice Schweitzer. "Don't Stop Believing: Rituals Improve Performance by Decreasing Anxiety." *Organizational Behavior and Human Decision Processes 137* (November 2016): 71–85.

Burns, D. D. *Feeling Good: The New Mood Therapy.* Read by George Newbern. Harper Audio, 2017.

Carnegie, D., D. D. Carnegie, and L. Thomas. *How to Win Friends and Influence People: Updated for the Next Generation of Leaders.* Simon & Schuster, 2022.

Carney, D. R., A. J. C. Cuddy, and A. J. Yap. "Power Posing." *Psychological Science, 21*(10) (2010): 1363–1368. https://doi.org/10.1177/0956797610383437

Chand, S.P., D. P. Kuckel, and M.R. Huecker. "Cognitive Behavior Therapy." [Updated May 23, 2023]. In: StatPearls [Internet]. Treasure Island, FL: StatPearls Publishing. (January 2024). Available from: https://www.ncbi.nlm.nih.gov/books/NBK470241

Harvard Health. "Breath Meditation: A Great Way to Relieve Stress." (April 15, 2014). https://www.health.harvard.edu/mind-and-mood/breath-meditation-a-great-way-to-relieve-stress

Harvard Health. "The Healing Power of Art." (July 1, 2017). https://www.health.harvard.edu/mental-health/the-healing-power-of-art

Landefeld, J. C., C. Miaskowski, L. Tieu, C. Ponath, C. T. Lee, D. Guzman, and M. Kushel. "Characteristics and Factors Associated with Pain in Older Homeless Individuals: Results from the Health Outcomes in People Experiencing Homelessness in Older Middle Age (HOPE HOME) Study." *The Journal of Pain, 18*(9) (2017): 1036–1045. https://doi.org/10.1016/j.jpain.2017.03.011

Mayo Foundation for Medical Education and Research. "Being Assertive: Reduce Stress, Communicate Better." Mayo Clinic. (January 20, 2024b). https://www.mayoclinic.org/healthy-lifestyle/stress-management/in-depth/assertive/art-20044644

Rossignol, M., S.-A. Fisch, P. Maurage, F. Joassin, and P. Philippot. "Reduced Processing of Facial and Postural Cues in Social Anxiety: Insights from Electrophysiology." *Plos One, 8*(9) (2013). https://doi.org/10.1371/journal.pone.0075234

Singh, R. K., B. J. Voggeser, and A. S. Göritz. "Beholden: The Emotional Effects of Having Eye Contact While Breaking Social Norms." *Frontiers in Psychology, 12* (2021). https://doi.org/10.3389/fpsyg.2021.545268

Tartakovsky, M. "How to Deal with an Especially Cruel Inner Critic." Psych Central. (October 2, 2018). https://psychcentral.com/blog/how-to-deal-with-an-especially-cruel-inner-critic

Thompson, T., N. Van Zalk, C. Marshall, et al. "Social Anxiety Increases Visible Anxiety Signs during Social Encounters but Does Not Impair Performance." *BMC Psychology 7*, 24 (2019). https://doi.org/10.1186/s40359-019-0300-5

The University of Texas Permian Basin. "How Much of Communication Is Nonverbal?" (May 15, 2023). https://online.utpb.edu/about-us/articles/communication/how-much-of-communication-is-nonverbal

Resources

The Art of Communicating by Thich Nhat Hanh. A profound guide on effective communication, helping you connect deeply with yourself and others.

The Creative Cure: How Finding and Freeing Your Inner Artist Can Heal Your Life by Jacob Nordby. Discover how embracing your creativity can lead to profound healing and personal growth.

Dare to Lead by Brené Brown. Brown shares how being brave and real can make you a better leader. She gives simple advice on accepting flaws, understanding others, and building strong relationships to boost your confidence in social situations.

Feeling Good: The New Mood Therapy by David D. Burns. A self-help book that offers practical techniques to overcome depression and develop a positive outlook on life.

The Gifts of Imperfection by Brené Brown. This book explores how embracing our vulnerabilities can lead to a more fulfilling life.

How to Be Yourself: Quiet Your Inner Critic and Rise Above Social Anxiety by Ellen Hendriksen. Practical advice on overcoming social anxiety and embracing your true self.

The Happiness Trap: 8-Week Program. A (paid) program based on "Acceptance and Commitment Therapy" (ACT) to help reduce stress and increase life satisfaction. The website also offers free resources. https://thehappinesstrap.com/

"How to Be More Assertive—7 Tips." A YouTube video by The Distilled Man to deepen your understanding and enhance your assertiveness skills. This video offers insightful, actionable guidance complemented by real-life examples that illustrate how to apply assertiveness in various situations effectively. https://www.youtube.com/watch?v=NBkvWCmz2W4

Mind. Mind is a leading mental health charity providing advice and support to empower anyone experiencing a mental health problem. They offer fantastic resources for self-care, practical advice, and support groups to help you stay on track. www.mind.org.uk

The Mindful Movement. This YouTube channel offers guided meditations designed to help you find inner peace through a soothing visualization. Perfect for moments of stress or anxiety.

"The Power of Vulnerability." A TED Talk by Brené Brown. An inspiring talk that delves into the importance of vulnerability and authenticity in our lives. https://www.ted.com/talks/brene_brown_the_power_of_vulnerability

Index

Acknowledgments

Writing this book has been one of the most rewarding experiences of my life, and I am deeply grateful to everyone who played a part in its creation.

First and foremost, my heartfelt thanks go to Lonnie Mullet. Your unwavering support and guidance have been a beacon of light, helping me navigate the complexities of becoming a therapist. Your wisdom and encouragement have shaped me into the professional I am today, and I am eternally grateful.

To my close group of therapist colleagues, your constant support, insightful feedback, and shared experiences have been invaluable. You have enriched my work in ways words cannot fully express, and I am deeply thankful for your camaraderie and wisdom.

Nicole Newell, your mentorship has been a cornerstone of my journey. Your expertise, patience, and constructive feedback have helped me refine my ideas and enhance the quality of my writing. Your belief in me has been a source of strength, and I cannot thank you enough.

To my friends and family, your unwavering love and encouragement have been the foundation on which I stand. You believed in me even when I doubted myself, and your support has been a constant source of motivation. I am profoundly grateful for your endless faith in my abilities.

To my clients, thank you for sharing your stories and experiences. Your courage and resilience inspire me daily and drive my passion to continue this work. Your journeys have taught me much and fueled my commitment to helping others.

Finally, I extend my gratitude to the various institutions and experts in the field whose insights and knowledge have significantly informed my work. Your contributions have ensured its relevance and accuracy, and I sincerely appreciate your support.

Thank you all from the bottom of my heart. None of this would have been possible without each of you. Your belief, support, and contributions have made this dream a reality, and I am forever thankful.

About the Author

 **Megan Ashley Smith, LCMHC, NCC,** is a licensed clinical mental health therapist with a mission to help people overcome social anxiety and lead fulfilling lives. Having personally navigated the turbulent waters of social and general anxiety, she brings a deep sense of empathy and understanding to her practice, making her approach both relatable and compelling.

Megan's journey as a therapist has included work with adults, teens, and children. She finds immense joy in engaging with schools and leading therapeutic groups, where she's able to extend her reach and inspire positive change on a broader scale.

Outside the therapy room, her life is enriched by the companionship of her two beloved dogs, Guinness and Sage. Their playful energy and unconditional love are constant reminders of life's simple joys. Music is another cornerstone of her life—fueling her spirit and providing a comforting escape.

Mindfulness is Megan's anchor. It keeps her grounded and present, allowing her to navigate the complexities of life with grace and intention. This practice not only enhances her personal well-being, but also informs her therapeutic techniques by equipping her with effective tools to pass on to clients.

Megan's own experiences with social anxiety drive the desire to help others navigating the same rough road. She's dedicated to supporting others as they embark on their journey toward resilience, confidence, and joy.